fossils

of all ages

First published in the United States in 1978
by Grosset & Dunlap, Inc., 51 Madison Avenue
New York, 10010

Copyright © 1976 by Les Editions du Pacifique, Tahiti.
All rights reserved for all countries.
English translation ██████████ by Grosset & Dunlap, New York.
Originally published in French under the title Fossiles de tous les temps.

All rights reserved
Published simultaneously in Canada
Library of Congress catalog card number: 77-94513
ISBN 0-448-14718-1
First printing 1978
Printed and bound in Japan

fossils
of all ages

by Jean-Claude Fischer and Yvette Gayrard-Valy

Preface by Jean Piveteau, Membre de l'Institut
Photographs by Denis Serrette and Rachid Kandaroun

from the collections of the National Museum of Natural History, Paris

GROSSET & DUNLAP
A FILMWAYS COMPANY
Publishers • New York

Contents

1
Spirifer mucronatus

Preface

This book by Jean-Claude Fischer and Yvette Gayrard-Valy is distinct from the many other publications on paleontology in presentation, content, form, and background. It involves a large and astonishing iconography, as well as commentary of the highest scientific rank. But above all, it contains reflections by the authors that will draw readers into meditation on the great problems suggested and encountered by the science of fossils.

Paleontology cannot avoid the law whose formulation it prompted—that a creature or thing can only be understood by understanding its history. Similarly, the spirit and structure of a science can only be grasped through knowledge of its development. *Fossils of All Ages* begins with an evocation of this past, with a tale of the human mind's uncertainty before the nature and meaning of fossils.

Science and the supernatural were often confused until the very end of the 18th century. In addition, following an old and powerful tradition, human science was regarded as theology's servant. Throughout the 18th century there were many "physical theologies," and the "theology of fossils" prospered. Following the authors' fascinating account, we watch paleontology winning its autonomy—slowly establishing its methods and finally presenting us with a new vision of the world. Thus we have not only a chapter in the history of science but an authentic contribution to the history of the human mind's understanding.

Fossils, as the material of paleontological study, are themselves a subject of wonder. Their existence presents us with a problem: how can a living creature retain its appearance, often to the smallest detail, while transforming itself into minerals?

The process of fossilization is usually described in a summary manner. Our authors have been able to show its importance and, after explaining the various modes of fossil formation, they have indicated how fossils are discovered and brought to light. Their vivid account of the great paleontological expeditions makes us sense, once again, the emotion stirred by these witnesses of the past which, beyond satisfying curiosity, allow us to feel that we can grasp life's processes through its creative efforts. Our vision of the contemporary world is also enriched: we see the variety of forms and structures that are always subject in their diversity to the laws of calculation and geometry, and the breadth of structural types that also respond to the exigencies of physical laws.

Naturally, such discoveries open up for the authors (and for the reader as well) the enigma unearthed by paleontology—the enigma of time, the universe's time as well as life's, and humanity's.

Clear and accurate, and written in a lively and vibrant style, this book presents a solid yet entertaining introduction to life's past, and suggests an opening onto its future. It will lead the reader to meditate the great questions of paleontological science: creation and evolution, origin and destiny.

Jean Piveteau
Membre de l'Institut

2

Completely silicified, this trunk from a tree fern (Psaronius Brasiliensis) has been preserved, after 250 million years, in its entire anatomical structure down to the smallest detail, as we can see from this polished transversal cut.

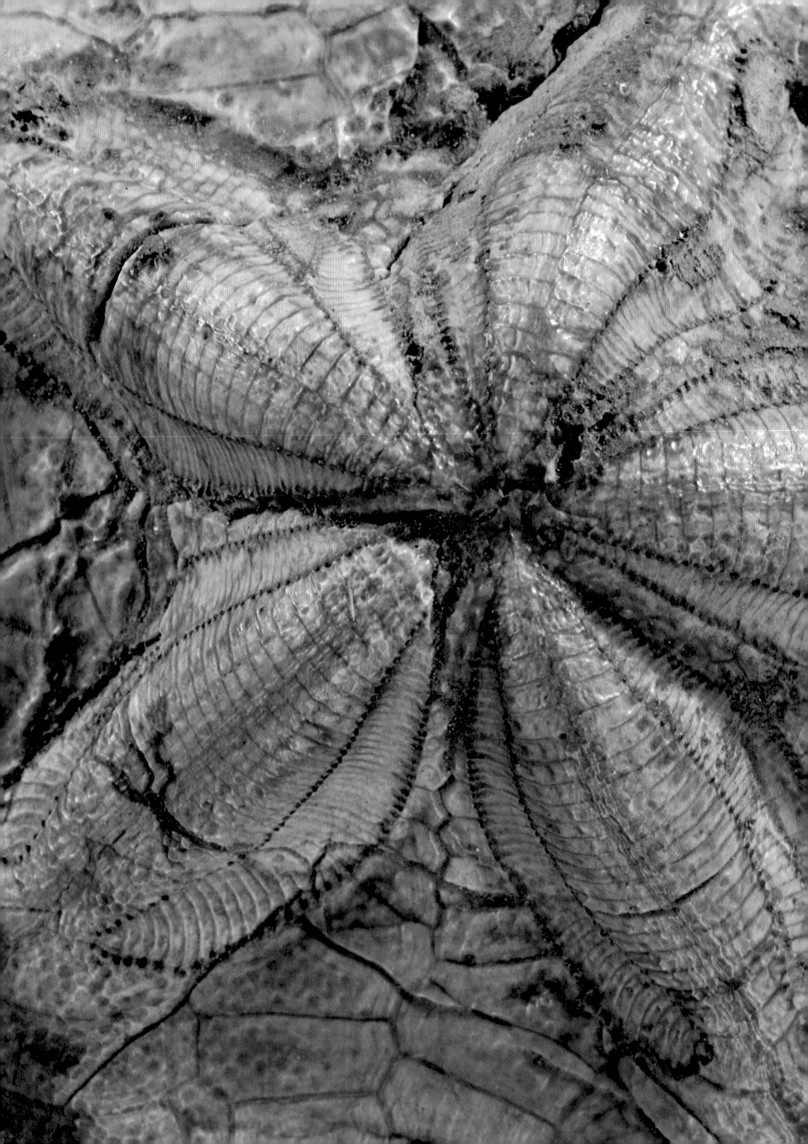

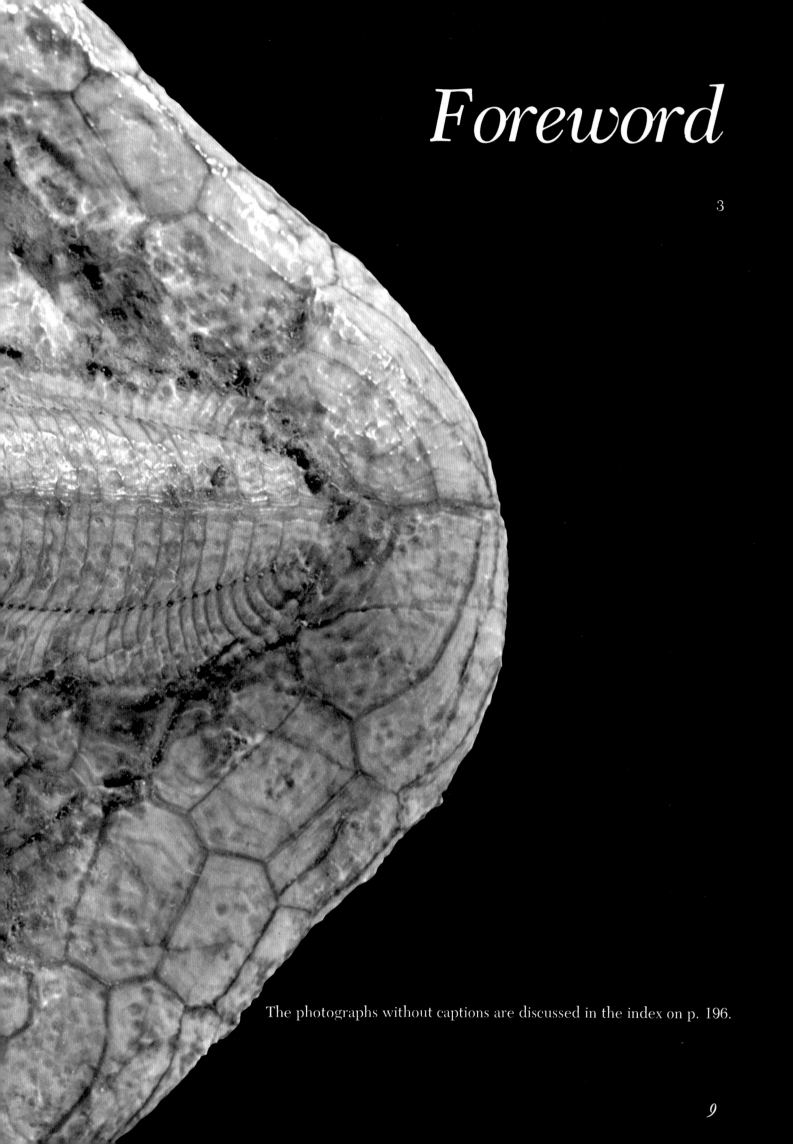

Foreword

3

The photographs without captions are discussed in the index on p. 196.

This is a book for all who, from a scientific, phenomenological, or purely aesthetic viewpoint, are interested in fossils, the witnesses of the biological past and revealers of the astonishing transformations that have marked life's evolution since its origin, and gradually fashioned the terrestrial world. It is not a treatise or atlas, but an "anthology" of the remarkable vestiges of life placed by geological deposits before our curious eyes. These are not necessarily "classic" forms, or the ones that interest specialists, but those that strike our sensibilities and imaginations through their evocative power, the balance of lines and volumes, the beauty of materials, and the revelations of the phenomena they display.

Thus, we will hardly touch on evolution, and still less on chronstratigraphy, treating systems (certain groupings of works) not at all. On these fascinating but traditional subjects of paleontology there are already many excellent books, geared for different levels of knowledge—designed to satisfy the most demanding or least informed readers. In contrast, however, few authors have concerned themselves with presenting fossils in light of their suggestive powers in the field of intellectual research and creativity.

We can measure the growing interest in the spectacle of plant and animal life by the numerous marvelously illustrated publications that depict the splendors of nature. Beside these living species, which are usually familiar, fossils seem rare things, treasured objects. We are actually dealing with species that, because they are extinct, cannot be renewed, with species whose interesting specimens, since they are fixed in limited quantities in sedimentary rocks, form the exception rather than the rule.

The beauties of fossil nature seem to have been forgotten, or neglected. This is a gap which we have long had the urge to fill.

It is common to say that a botanist does not look at plants with the eyes of an artist. Nor does a paleontologist usually have the same view of fossils as an amateur. The specialization required by modern scientific research frequently hides the evocative value of its objects. Rigor and objectivity are usually the specialist's prime goals, and may cause him to neglect or at least not to express the aesthetics of the vegetable and animal worlds, so that he often regards an organism's body or form as a mere "physical sack," as the art historian Henri Focillon observed. Morphological characteristics have, nevertheless, an aesthetic value that determines the originality of each object. This is the "representative value" which the biologist Adolphe Portmann discussed, stressing "the importance of external form, which the quest for directly vital functions has often caused us to neglect."

Most works of scientific specialization—and of paleontology in particular—take dissemination of knowledge as their end, and provide illustrations only to facilitate understanding the text. The present work takes a totally different—almost opposite—approach. The reader is invited to study the most beautiful fossils of all time with an eye to their aesthetic value. The commentaries on the illustrations will teach the origin of each form, its age, its mode of life, and how it was fossilized. Thus, if the reader's interest leads him or her to learn more, the footnotes are there as guides. The text will not provide exact scientific knowledge but will give general ideas designed to familiarize one with the many lessons fossils involve. And if an aspect of paleontology should attract attention, it will be easy for the reader to extend his or her knowledge by the varied documentary sources available.

This book is thus a work of inspiration, deliberately placed on a cultural rather than a purely scientific level.

This book could not have been possible without the willing aid of all those whose help and participation we needed. To them we express our most grateful thanks, and particularly to the following:

Professor J. P. Lehman, M. J. Sornay, Mrs. C. Blanc, M. L. Ginsburg, Mrs. M. Deflandre-Riguad, Mrs. Y. Le Calvez, J. P. Chevalier, J. Blot, E. Buge, Mrs. F. Debrenne, Miss J. Drot, D. Heyler, M. Dutuit, J. Roman, D. Goujet, and Mrs. M. Gaudant (Paleontology Institute of the Museum, Paris).

We also wish to thank Professor R. Laffitte, Miss D. Noel, F. Gautier, J. P. Caulet, Y. Reyre (Geological Laboratory of the Museum, Paris), Professor J. Fabries, M. H. Schubnel (Minerological Laboratory of the Museum, Paris), Miss S. Kelner-Pillault (Entomology Laboratory of the Museum, Paris), Professor J. Guiart, Mrs. M. de Fontanes, and Mrs. S. Thierry (Museum of Man, Paris).

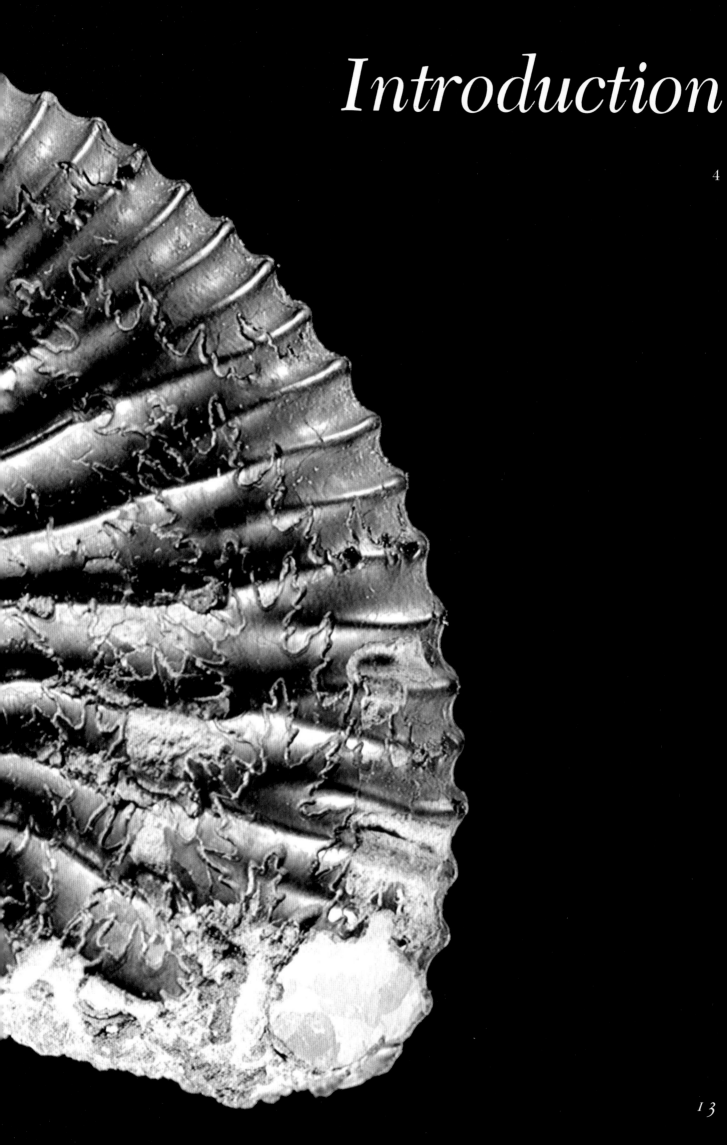

Introduction

4

The archaeologist always finds the most reliable witnesses of past civilizations in the ground—in cut stones and hardened imprints preserved from dispersion and change by sediments. Thus he has been able to extricate vestiges of Nineveh, Delphi, and ancient Rome which have been preserved in all their living reality for many millennia after their inhabitants ceased to animate them.

Similarly, by methodical excavation of the oldest lands, the prehistorian can unearth traces and fossilized witnesses of the first human antecendents, and revive the astonishing development of our furthest ancestors: Australopithecans with low foreheads, who appeared over three billion years ago and were succeeded by Pithecanthropan tribes, and then Neanderthal societies, before modern humanity made its appearance over 37,000 years ago. But the earth encloses in its "archives" documents of life's development that date from even more distant epochs. Long before infant humanity cast the first strokes of its prodigious development, the oceans and continents were already populated by a multitude of animal and plant species, whose remains the paleontologist finds buried in geological sediments. These vestiges, called *fossils*, form the basis of our knowledge of the extraordinary evolution of living phenomena over more than three billion years. Regarded by some as simple natural curiosities, by others as collectibles or objects of scientific study, fossils have always fascinated humanity by their strangeness and antiquity, and by the information they bring us about our planet's evolution. They are preserved for us by nature in the most diverse forms, sometimes intact down to the smallest details as if almost alive, sometimes reduced to the state of fragments, imprints, or simple traces. These traces are usually from the "hard parts"—shells, carapaces, scales, teeth, or bones.

We know some so strange they seem to have come from other planets.

Others are disturbing and must have troubled our most distant ancestors who had to live among them.

Some are horrific, causing us to ask what fantasy or curious caprice might have driven nature to produce such creatures.

But there are others, as well, which are works of art.

Nature herself knows neither beauty nor ugliness, good nor evil. What matters in the plant and animal worlds is the ability to endure, to multiply, to adapt. Notions of beauty and ugliness, indeed, are the creations of the human psyche. We appreciate the qualities of volume, form, and proportion, such as texture, color, sound and its harmony, according to the knowledge, habit, or use we make of them, or according to the sense of security we can derive from them. From this harmonic relation of form to function we draw, certainly, our notion of a living thing's beauty. Ugliness, in contrast, is usually suggested by the strange, abnormal, or disquieting cast of certain creatures or objects. What we call "prehistoric" animals or plants are usually ones we have never seen alive, which are foreign to our humanized world and which evoke terrifying and inhospitable epochs.

What, then, forms the beauty of fossils? On such a topic every individual has his or her own standards and values, according to knowledge, imagination, and involvement with the animal, vegetable, and mineral worlds. For us, as geologists and paleontologists who are scientifically acquainted with these precursors of living flora and fauna, the finest fossils will be those revealing the most about the remarkable adventure in which all human past and future is involved. This adventure is dominated by permanent contradictions between the fragility and power of life, between its fugitive nature and its endurance, between smallness and grandeur, in an endless renewal of abilities and forms, inventions and conquests. For all those intrigued by them, the finest fossils will also be ones evoking reflection on our evolutionary perception of the world, on the relativity of terrestrial time, the dynamics of living phenomena, and the slow elaboration, inestimable value, and precariousness of our current biological environment.

5

6

7 8

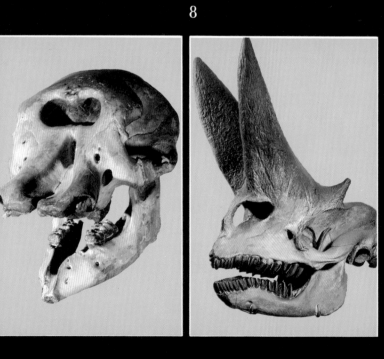

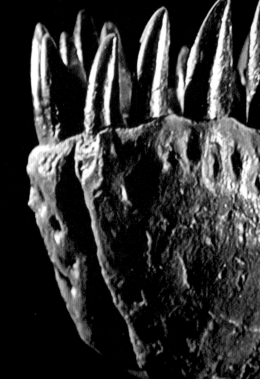

1. Fossils: Witnesses to the Biological Past

What view of the living world could we have without the lessons of fossils? What would our notion of the beginnings of plants, animals, and man be? Probably somewhat like that of most of the great minds of the early nineteenth century—a vision of a nature of recent descent, set into motion once and for all, complete, fixed, and finalized. From this point of view, we would infer that the living world has but a small capacity for evolution and that it has been in the process of decline—witness the recent and predictable extinction of many species. We would also deduce that all living species, including man, were the same age and would consequently suppose them to be of directly creative origin. Without knowledge of fossils, our philosophical systems would have borrowed other sails, and our spiritual orientation would be totally different. To convince ourselves we need only measure the resonance that the irrefutable proofs of man's prehistoric origins, the agedness of life, and its slow evolution over three billion years have had on Western thought, and particularly on Christian dogmatism.

Great paleontological discoveries have similarly served to orient the earth and life sciences, which currently rely on lessons from the fossil world to buttress theories or clarify their demonstrations. Mining industries have, on their own, benefitted from the progress of paleontology. Paleontology has made important contributions to the development of the modern economy by directing prospecting and facilitating the exploitation of hydrocarbons, coal, and many other mineral beds.

The science of the biological past, paleontology remains a perfectly contemporary science, as much through the importance of its research, teachings, and their applications as through the role it plays in knowledge and culture. Younger than geology, botany, or zoology, it figures among the newest of the great scientific disciplines. Thus, though the existence of fossils has been known since Aristotle's time, there are still many surprises in store.

The First Discoveries and Attempts at Their Interpretation

Since the beginning of time, man has recognized—whether imprisoned in sediment or embedded in solid rock—the remains of living beings that have been largely transformed into stone. Marine shells were the most plentiful and the easiest to identify, and their presence in paleolithic burial places proves that the first men already accorded them some significance.

Greek antiquity is rich in indications of interest in fossils, and in attempts to explain their origins. Thales (640–548 B.C.) was one of the first authors to concern himself with the earth's make-up, and his disciple Anaximander (610–547 B.C.) mentions discoveries of shells and marine remains in the mountains—the imprints of fish found in rocks at Samos and in Sicily. These were proof, he said, of ancient oceans long since "burned out" by the sun. Pythagoras (580–500 B.C.), cited by Ovid in his *Metamorphoses*, was in turn to observe, "I have seen lands flowing from the heart of the waves; far distant from the sea were embedded marine shells." Xenophon (580–490 B.C.) maintained that earth and water, which were intermingled in primitive times, had gradually separated into oceans and continents; the proof being that "shells are found in the wide earth and in mountains."

As for the philosopher and doctor Empedocles (484–424 B.C.), he noted hippopotamus bones in Sicily and mistook them for the bones of vanished giants. Empedocles' contemporary, Herodotus (484–425 B.C.), who scaled the mountains of Egypt and the Libyan desert, noted the presence of shells and thought that "Egypt might have been a gulf, carrying the Mediterranean waters as far as Ethiopia."

Thus, the first observations concluded with an organic origin for fossils which, in the final analysis, was perhaps the most logical one. This was one of the merits of Greek science. Unfortunately other theories, appealing to more confused causes, were soon to be composed.

A century after Herodotus, Aristotle (384–322 B.C.), studying the Nile delta, recognized that "It is not always the same pieces of Earth which we find under water, nor the same on dry land . . . these regions do not remain oceans, nor those firm land." But Aristotle, who believed in spontaneous generation, had a very clear idea about the origin of fossils. He thought that exhalations rose from the earth in sunlight, with the "humid" ones producing metals and the "dry" ones fossils! His scientific ideas, taken up by Arab commentators, were centuries later, to become the foundations of medieval science.

One of Aristotle's contemporaries and disciples, Theophrastus of Lesbos (372–287 B.C.), articulated an even stranger theory: "The earth produces bones and is formed of bony rocks." All theory of organic origin is thus swept aside by this new theory which unfortunately made its way into the Middle Ages and far later.

In any case, at the dawn of the Christian era the Greek geographer Strabo (58 B.C.–A.D. 25), was once more to seek a plausible explanation of fossil origins. Greek scientific thought stopped with him, and the Latins Lucretius, Horace, and Ovid, more poets than observers, were content to take up the Greek ideas again. Pliny the Ancient (A.D. 23–79) shared Theophrastus' baffling scientific opinions. In his *Natural History*, he mentions certain fossils—the "ostracites" in the shape of oysters, and "spongites" in sponge form. But he takes the teeth of fossil sharks for petrified tongues, calling them *Glossopetrae*, a name they would keep for centuries: "The glossopetra falls from the sky during the moon's eclipses." In contrast, Pliny was one of the first to guess the true nature of amber, "a marrow flowing from a kind of pine." After him, several last and wholly unoriginal hypotheses joined those of the early Greeks. For a long time no new curiosity would renew the interest in these objects of nature and the knowledge of fossils would founder for centuries in obscurantism and superstition.

The Nature and Legendary Properties of Fossils

Ambiguous objects, sharing both living form and stone, fossils were destined to be sources of legends. Many of these beliefs arose in the ancient world of the Middle Ages, and were maintained through succeeding centuries. To this day, some fossils keep magical properties for certain nonscientific civilizations, or according to folklore.

Thus, for the ancients, fossilized sea-urchins were stones that had fallen during thunder and rain, or were thought to be "Serpent's eggs," formed by entangled reptiles, which then supposedly protected them from lightning, venom, and poison. Their prickles were called "Judaic stone" (the first ones were brought back from Judea), Syrian stones, or "St. Paul's staff," and cured "disorders of the bladder and kidneys."

Shark's teeth, those famous *Glossopetrae*, were "lightning stings" or the petrified tongues of Maltese serpents, used for curing snake bites,

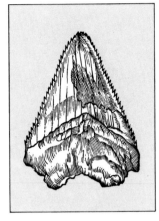

10

Until the eighteenth century sharks' teeth were taken for petrified snakes' tongues, or Glossopetrae. Pliny believed that they had fallen from the sky during a lunar eclipse. This one was depicted by Aldrovandri in 1648 in his Museum metallicum.

11

Popular superstition has always conferred supernatural powers on fossils. These nineteenth-century Italian amulets arrange mammal teeth, madrepores, and a prehistoric arrowhead without discrimination.

vomiting, and malignant fevers. For a long time fossil madrepores (a type of coral) were called "stellar stones," or "Astroids"; they were also seen as "sacred agates," extracted from the head of an Indian dragon. They were said to cure plague, apoplexy, and liver and lung ailments, and to ward off venomous beasts.

Belemnites incited a lively curiosity from antiquity onward. Taken for "thunder stones," arrowheads turned into stone, or petrified lynx urine, they were called "fingers of Mt. Ida," "devil's fingers," or "fingers of St. Peter." The name belemnite, from the Greek *Belemnon* meaning in the form of a javelin, was given them by Agricola in 1546 B.C. They were long sought by apothecaries.

Ammonites, called "Ammon's horns" from their resemblance to a goat's horn, were "the form in which Jupiter was worshipped in the Egyptian desert." They were also taken for curling serpents changed into stone by the English abbess St. Hilda. Folklore long attributed to them specific therapeutic properties.

Fossil mollusks and brachiopods were sought for magical purposes. In Southern Morocco they were used for fortune-telling and worn as amulets. In England, the fossil oyster *Gryphaea arcuata* was called "the devil's signature," and was employed to cure arthritis and bone illnesses. The shell marls of Touraine were the object of religious customs and folklore until the last century. Even in our day, fossil brachiopods figure in children's games throughout the Swiss countryside.

Accumulations of *Nummulites*, which are abundant in certain limestones, became "money stones," or "farthing stones," the Sphinx's coins in Egypt, witch's change in Spain, St. Peter's or the devil's money in France. In Central Europe these were "coins petrified by a Miracle so as to stun the enemy's eyes and save those in flight."

Amber has since antiquity occupied a privileged place: as hardened lynx urine, "sap of sunshine," the tears of Meleagridean birds, or of Nymphs changed into poplars and bemoaning the stricken Phaeton. It was called Electrum (from one of the sun's names, Elector) or Succin, from the belief that it was melted by the sun's rays and solidified by the sea. Its innumerable medicinal properties were much respected up to the eighteenth century. Amber, said a chronicler, "is good for tearing eyes, for the heart, brain illnesses, shortened breath, stones, dropsy, circulation, toothache, menstrual periods, pregnancy, gout, epilepsy, catarrhes (the common cold), aching joints, stomach ache, plague, nightmares

12

Translucent and strange in color, amber was for a long time thought to be divinely created. Collectors have always sought this fossil resin. Baltic amber, the most abundant, contains marvelous specimens of fossil insects.

. . . it is an antidote for poison and stops hemorrhaging . . . it makes fevers subside." In short, "its powers are so miraculous that it might be termed the balm of Europe."

The fossilized remains of large extinct vertebrates fed legends of terrifying animals with supernatural powers. The Quaternary period saw the extinction of giant birds that in turn animated Egyptian, Chinese, Arabian, Madagascan, and New Zealander legends. The bones of large fossil mammals, particularly the proboscidians, were for a long time taken for the remains of giants who had peopled the ancient world. The crania of Quaternary elephants found in Sicily were apparently responsible for the origin of the Cyclops legend, their singular nasal orifice having inspired the idea of an enormous frontal eye. Orion's skeleton was thought to have been discovered in Crete, and Ajax's at Salamine. Boccaccio recounts the discovery of Polyphemus' body. Elephants' molars unearthed here and there helped reinforce this belief in France, Switzerland, and Germany.

For a long time the tusks of fossil proboscidians were thought to be unicorns' horns containing strong medicinal properties; for this reason the pharmacy at the Court of Würtenberg bought sixty of them in the year 1700. Many Siberian and Manchu legends were inspired by discoveries of remains of mammoths frozen in ice. They tell the tale of a giant rat, a mythic being living under the ice and provoking earth tremors when it moved, which died as soon as it saw daylight.

In the plant kingdom, the trucks of silicified trees scattered over the Arizona landscape were believed by the Indians to be either the bones of a gigantic monster or the broken arms left from a battle between gods and giants.

There are numerous other examples of the role played by fossils in legends and superstition. We cannot dwell further on them here. But it is an extremely rich field whose exploration would be fascinating.

"Nature's Games," or "Failed Attempts at Creation"

Shaken by the barbarian invasions and swayed by religious preoccupations in which whatever did not adhere strictly to Christian doc-

13

Noted since antiquity, sharks' teeth are found in many sites in remarkable states of preservation. These are from the Peruvian site Sacaco, and date from the Upper Miocene.

Ophiomorphites.

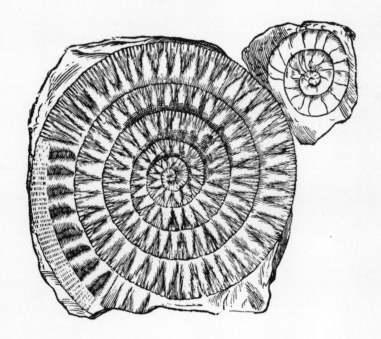

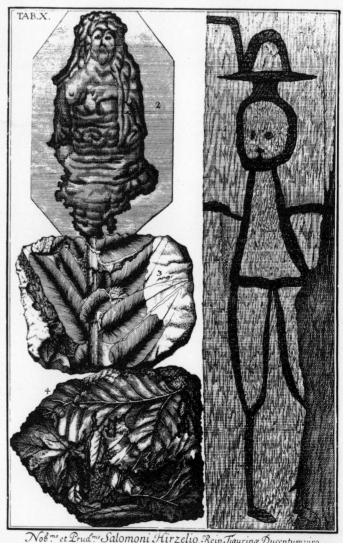

TAB. X.

Nob.mo et Prud.mo Salomoni Hirzelio, Reip.Tigurinæ Ducentumviro,
Venerab. Collegii Examinatorum Assessori, Amico optimo. Huber, del. et Sculp.

trines was condemned, Western medieval science showed no interest whatsoever in the earth's history or fossil knowledge. It was the Arabs, in the full flowering of their civilization, who first gathered and translated the ancient texts. Only through the conquest of northern Africa and the Iberian peninsula were the science of the past and philosophy able to penetrate the West.

A Persian doctor and philosopher, Avicenna (930–1037), was the first to reinstate Aristotle's doctrines. In his treatise *De Minerabilis* he recognized the living origin of fossils, but explained their transformation into stone as a "mineralizing property," the *Vis lapidifica*, of primitive clay. Teaching Aristotle's philosophy, which the Christian community thought dangerous, was forbidden in 1215. But in 1231 his works on the natural sciences were edited and taught at the University of Paris, and his *Meteorology* became the basis for medieval geology.

In turn, the Dominican Albert the Great (1193–1280), a man of science as well as a theologian, translated and commented on the ancient texts. In his work of 1260, *De Mineralibus et Rebus metallicis*, he recognized, agreeing with Avicenna, that "animals can be entirely transformed into stone," and he attributed the "mineralizing property" (*vis lapidifica* or *virtu formativa*) to the sun and the stars.

Up to this point the organic nature of fossils was never contested. But already an irrational element was penetrating the scientific universe. Little by little it would alter its nature entirely.

Belief in celestial influence was to know numerous adherents like the fourteenth century Nicolo Manetti. On finding a series of plant imprints, Manetti wrote: "through the course of time and under the action of the sun and other celestial bodies, these parts of the earth have gradually become stone." In the early sixteenth century George Bauer, called Agricola (1494–1555), stated that plants and animals had become petrified through the action of a *succus lapidescens* (*De natura fossilium*, 1546). During the same epoch, the anatomist Gabriel Fallopio (1525–1562) thought that fossils had been formed by "terrestrial exhalations."

14, 15, 16

For many centuries fossils were interpreted in a highly fantastical manner. Examples are this ammonite and fish from Aldrovandi's Museum metallicum *(1648) and the plate from Scheuchzer's* Herbarium diluvianum *(1723), in which scrupulous observation coexists with delirious imagination.*

Such attempts at explanation continued throughout the seventeenth century. People spoke of "sap" with "the power of petrification," of "assimilating powers" or "petrifying powers." And as for the origin of such organic remains, they were supposed to arise from "seeds" which, by "their small size and the help of the waters," had penetrated the "earth's entrails," where subterranean heat had made them grow and then perish, leaving their imprints behind. Such was the opinion of Edward Lwhyd, who in 1699 published a description of sixteen hundred English animal and plant fossils. In the same spirit, G. F. Maraldi wrote in 1706, "there are subterranean Fish just as subterranean waters."

And so they were to return to Aristotle's theories of spontaneous generation, stated 2000 years before! L. Bourget said in 1729: "So as to explain the origin of these Fossils, Philosophers have had recourse to alchemy, to the Archinobolic and Formative powers, to sigillary (occult) Ideas, germinal forces, and a hundred other like Agents. . ."

Other pseudo-scientific notions went further still, totally ignoring organic fossil origin. Thus fossils were thought to have been spontaneously formed at the earth's core by a *vis plastica*, if they did not result from the fermentation of a *materia pinguis* in the rocks' interior. In the seventeenth century, the Englishman Martin Lister wrote: "These shell-shaped stones have always been just what they presently are, *lapides sui generis* and never any animal part whatsoever." In 1708, the Swiss doctor Karl Nikolaus Lang spoke of fossils which he called "figured stones." Fossils are no longer more than simple "games of nature," *ludens naturae*, the curious accidents of chance. In 1700, the English doctor Charles Leigh would go so far as to consider as such an elephant skeleton discovered in 1696 in Thuringia!

These "figured stones" were studied along with minerals and rocks. Mingled with superstition, purely imaginary figurations—demonic ones—were added. In the *Mundi subterranei* published in 1678 by Athanase Kircher, the natural sciences are seen as neighbors of alchemy, and fossils the relatives of dragons. Organic remains were considered the Creator's "failures," possibly made by Satan measuring himself against God.

Once more everything was thrown into question. In 1766 E. Bertrand was not afraid to write that "fossil debris are figured stones buried in the soil by God, who wished to place more harmony in his works, more correspondence between things living in the waters and on earth and those which must be underground." Voltaire himself in his *Philosophical Questions* was to pose this curious query: "Can one really be sure that the Earth's soil cannot give birth to fossils?"

Fossils and the Flood

Another current of thought acknowledged fossils as the unquestioned remains of living beings, petrified in a natural manner. This opinion, put to rest since the time of the ancient Greeks, took on new vigor but was unhappily deflected by Christian influence, which brought with it belief in the Biblical flood. According to this, the shells and fish found at the summits of mountains were proof of a general inundation.

One of the main authors who was drawn to geology was the thirteenth century Italian, Ristoro D'Arezzo. In his *Composizione del Mondo* (1282), he notes: "in scouring a very tall mountain up to its summit, we have found a large quantity of these fish bones . . . along with sands and rounded stones . . . mingled from place to place as if they had been deposited by a river. This is a certain sign that the mountain was made by the Flood." The notion of the Flood soon became firmly established, pursuing its own course of development parallel to theories of spontaneous generation. But it was in the seventeenth and above all the eighteenth centuries, when works on the natural sciences became abundant and began to be specialized, that biblical notions were to wield such influence that one can accurately speak of a "school of the Flood."

The Swiss naturalist Johan–Jacob Scheuchzer (1672–1733) was one of its most avid partisans. In 1708 he wrote that fossils "are not nature's toys, but belong to the animal kingdom," originating from the biblical Flood. His evidence was the discovery in 1726, in a quarry near Constance, of a stone fragment "on which one could distinguish perfectly the many parts of a human head." Scheuchzer enumerates all its bones, naming his fossil *Homo diluvii testis*. For him, "the truth of the Universal Flood, acknowledged for numerous centuries, has never been clearer than now." It was necessary to wait until 1787 for the anatomist Camper to recognize these famous remains as a "petrified lizard;" in 1825, Cuvier finally confirmed that it was but "an Aquatic Salamander of gigantic size and unknown species."

Meanwhile, the English doctor John Woodward (1665–1722) edited a *Natural History of the Earth*, followed by an *Essay on the History of the Fossils of England*. According to him, "the entire mass of the globe was dissolved and penetrated by shells."

This was the epoch of the multiplication of discoveries, not only in shells and fish relics, but also in the bones and teeth of large vertebrates. In France in 1729, Louis Bourget printed a *Memory on the theory of the Earth's formation*, and in 1742 a *Treatise on Petrifications*, in which he categorically refuted spontaneous generation. He abandoned himself to numerous sharp observations on the sedimentation of soils and the novelty of certain fossil types that today are extinct. Unfortunately, he made no further innovations, and his conclusions are infected by the pseudo-scientific speculations of the period. For him, the proper explanation of fossil dispersion was "one which attributes their displacement and transport to an inundation of our entire globe comparable to the Flood whose history is preserved for us in the Sacred Writings." This theory of universal catastrophy had as its cause divine anger at the first men's corruption; the preservation of fossils was a warning for "Inhabitants of the Second Earth."

Such whimsical philosophical speculations had a great vogue during much of the eighteenth century, when they were taken up by Argenville in his *Oryctology*, a voluminous book treating "earth, stones, metals, and other fossils" which appeared in 1755. Today we are not astonished at the importance given to hypotheses that seem more theological than scientific. In any case, other opinions whetted by a vivid curiosity and firm observation have developed. They were gradually to lead fossil study and the history of the earth to their true scientific conclusions.

The Birth and Development of Paleontology

At the beginning of the thirteenth century, the English Franciscan monk Roger Bacon encouraged research and experimentation in his *Opus majus*, warning against unreserved acceptance of the ancients' thought and thus opening the door to a new science. By this time the different theories on the formation of mountains and sedimentary deposits had been widely discussed. The geological ideas of Albert de Saxe, Rector of

17

In 1648, Ulisse Aldrovandi of Bologna published the Museum metallicum, in which he displayed, along with minerals, crystals, and all kinds of concretions, many invertebrate fossils, and even elephant teeth, attributing to each the most surprising powers.

the University of Paris in 1357, were to influence Leonardo da Vinci (1452–1519), who was drawn for proof to the study of fossils. The first serious scientific position arose from the genius of Leonardo; he refuted both the spontaneous generation of fossils in earth, and the intervention of the Flood. Unfortunately, da Vinci's theories bore little fruit in Italy. Yet when fossil shells were unearthed during construction of the citadel of Verona, in 1517, the physician Girolamo Frascatoro grasped that they belonged to "real and true marine animals" that had lived on the same site.

Arising from Frascatoro's motivation, the first natural science collections began in Italy. The rich collection of Pope Sixtus V was studied and catalogued in 1574 by Michel Mercati under the name *Metallotheca Vaticana*. Soon other collections began to see the light of day, like that of Ulisse Aldrovandi, catalogued around 1585 as *Museum metallicum*.

In the same period, the Frenchman Bernard Palissy (1510–1590), "a simple potter knowing neither Latin nor Greek," scoured the Saintonge, the Touraine, the Ardennes, Champagne, going east to the banks of the Rhine and north as far as the Netherlands. He observed, collected, and sketched shells and "petrified" fish, identifying certain fossils with their current forms. Between 1575 and 1584 he came to Paris to tell all the capital savants that fossils were not, indeed, "nature's games," but the remains of living beings that had lived where the fossils were found "at the time when rocks were only water and silt." Palissy refuted spontaneous generation and any flood whatsoever. For this he received no credit and was imprisoned in the Bastille as a Huguenot.

Meanwhile the development of the miscroscope provided the natural sciences with a precious means of investigation. The microscope was invented in 1590 by Hans and Zacharias Janssen and used by Robert Hooke (1635–1703) to study small fossils like foraminifera and silicified wood fossils. To Hooke we can attribute the first evolutionary ideas: "Many varieties could have issued from the same species . . . for we know that variations in climate, soil, and nourishment often produce changes in the bodies which undergo them." The young science of paleontology was to profit greatly from this new orientation of thought.

During the same epoch, the Danish naturalist Nicolas Stenon (1638–1687) expressed the elementary principles of modern stratigraphy—deposit and superimposition of marine sediments, wrinklings, discordances, and the respective dating of these diverse phenomena.

Henceforth, the interpretation of fossils could be pursued according to a wholly different perspective, and above all could be chronologically ordered.

During the seventeenth century, fossils gradually began to move from the rank of objects of curiosity to one of objects of study. The number of important collections multiplied and their catalogues were published. But for the rational study of fossils, a means of classification permitting comparison of extinct and living forms was needed. The Swedish naturalist Carolus Linnaeus (1707–1778) defined the concepts of genera and species, and established "binomial nomenclature" (in which each individual is identified by its generic name followed by its species name), which is still used today. Hereafter, fossils were to take their place in the general classification of organized beings.

One problem was determining the actual age of fossils. Georges-Louis Leclerc de Buffon (1707–1788) was the first to infer the immense length of geological time. The author, in 1759, of *Theory of the Earth* and in 1778 of *Epochs of Nature*, Buffon wrote that "stratified beds result from sedimentation in waters, which is prolonged throughout millenia and not just the forty days of the Flood." Buffon confirmed that certain animal groups were exclusively fossil. This notion, once received, was instrumental in conceiving of the ladder of geological time.

Many naturalists, such as Alexandre Brongniart (1770–1847), were involved in establishing the relationship in time between fossils and their surrounding sedimentary rocks. Brongniart insisted that "formative epochs" were characterized by particular fossils, and stratigraphic paleontology was born.

Georges Cuvier (1769–1832) proposed an explanation of the differences between fossil and living organisms. In his *Discourse on the revolutions of the surface of the Globe* (1825), he wrote, "Life on this earth has often been troubled by terrible events. Innumerable living beings have been victims of these catastrophes." According to Cuvier, new populations developed between these brief "revolutions" which had made everything disappear. A pupil of Cuvier, Alcide d'Orbigny (1802–1857), also considered the founder of stratigraphic paleontology, decided that there were twenty-seven catastrophes on which to base his stages.

It is clear that attributing the differences between living and fossil forms to such a cause amounts to denying the possibility of evolution, since nothing links the different "creations" together. Thus Cuvier and

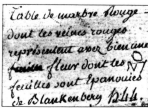

18

The poor state of scientific knowledge often led to naive descriptions like the one on this label written in 1836 for the polished section of Aulopora serpens, *a coral from the Devonian period in Germany. It says in part, "A slab of red marble."*

his disciples were given the name of the Fixist school.

Happily, Cuvier was a remarkable anatomist and the first naturalist to note the correlations linking the different organs of the same being, as well as to establish correspondences between organs of different creatures: "each type could, if need be, be recognized by each fragment of each of its parts." This comparative method, applied to the skeleton and proceeding by analogies, was to permit the reconstruction of extinct vertebrates. In 1812, Cuvier published his celebrated *Researches on the Fossil Bones of Quadrupeds*, in which he founds comparative anatomy and vertebral paleontology, a true science at last.

A New Vision of the World

The English geologist Charles Lyell (1797–1875) dealt Cuvier's "catastrophism" a mortal blow by showing that every transformation marked by geological strata could be shown to have arisen from the most ordinary causes, since the same phenomena had been active throughout the course of time. But it still remained for transformationist notions, whose germ was present in Buffon's work, to be concretized in evolutionist theories. The latter were to shake the foundations of an entire system of thought.

Jean-Baptiste Lamarck (1744–1829) first sensed the need to link living creatures to extinct ones. In his *Zoological Philosophy*, published in 1809, he established the derivation of all creatures from each other in a chain beginning with infusoria and larvae. Each modification of milieu prompted a parallel modification in the animal, which would then be transmitted through heredity: "All that nature causes an individual to acquire or lose . . . through the influence of the main usage of an organ or a continual defect in this part's use is conserved through generation in the resulting new individuals." For Lamarck there were no catastrophes or ruptures, but rather a continuum extending to the present day. This theory, based on the inheritance of acquired characteristics, was to be one of Charles Darwin's sources. Darwin, in contrast, did not attribute the modification of a species to morphological adaptation, but to a process of natural selection by which the best adapted species were the sole survivors. He expounded this doctrine in his work on *The origin of* species through the means of natural selection or the fight for existence in nature, which appeared in 1859.

While Lamarck had no audience among his contemporaries, Darwin found immediate success among the scientists of his time. Yet his theories unleashed tempests of protest from the many minds unprepared to question the principle "uniting the Creation with its Creator," or to admit that man and the monkey might be related. The indignation reached its highest point in 1871 when Darwin, sustained by the scientific world, dared to publish *The Descent of Man.* He was reproached for shedding doubt on the special status accorded man by God.

Darwin's work, which incited "an explosive mixture of anger, surprise, and wonder," had incalculable effects on the spiritual as well as the scientific levels. With time and the multiplication of works on the origin of the species, evolutionary lines, and man's predecessors, people began to see that evolutionary theories questioned not only the strict interpretation of many passages of Genesis, but also notions such as free will (for which the deterministic principle was generally substituted), human monogenesis (to which the principle of polygenism was opposed), and the idea of a "physical limit" between man and animal, which contradicted the reality of human evolution since the time of Australopithecus.

All contemporary thought, like all modern science, is more or less directly influenced by the strong thrust of transformationism, the generator of a new view of the world—the evolutionary view. As soon as the idea of evolution was accepted, man became aware that everything in the universe was endlessly evolving: space and energy, material and life, and man. The great modern theories were soon to be established.

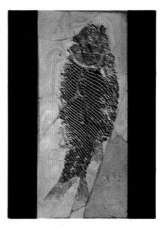

19

Lepidotes elvensis, *a bony fish from the Liassic in Germany. This genus disappeared at the end of the Cretaceous period and forms an intermediary stage preceding the modern fish. This specimen is remarkable for the fine preservation of its scales.*

Modern Definitions

Exactly what do we mean by "fossil"?

From the time of the Latin empire until the end of the eighteenth century, fossils were qualified as anything extracted from the earth, whether mineral substances (*fossilia nativa*) or organic bodies (*fossilia petrificata*). Today the term designates nothing more specific than "witnesses of life dating from geological epochs." This includes remains of the organisms themselves, whether plant or animal, as well as the traces of

20, 21

Tracks left by a small stegocephalian (primitive amphibian) in the swampy mud covering the area around Lodève, France, during the Permian period. They give us a rare opportunity to observe the nature of fossil soil.

their activities (the residue of organic material, footprints, animal tracks, holes). As the field of geology stops, by convention, at the boundary of the historical epoch (around 4000 B.C.), we call any organic remains from beyond this limit "subfossil."

The study of fossils and the phenomena of fossilization is the proper domain of paleonotology (from παλαιος, ancient, ων, being, λόγος, discourse), which we divide today into three main branches: paleobotany for the plant kingdom, paleozoology for the animal kingdom, and human paleontology linked to the domain of prehistory. A new branch was born with micropaleontology, or the study of plant and animal fossil micro-organisms. Each of these branches is subdivided by specialists according to directions of research, field of study, or the interrelations among the varied disciplines: paleoecology is most concerned with the way of life of fossils and the reconstruction of their environments, paleobiogeography treats the distribution of organisms during different periods, paleobiology regroups our modern system of taxonomy according to the physiology of extinct species.

Contributions of Paleontology to the Earth and Life Sciences

Since its field of investigation includes both biological phenomena and their related sedimentation processes, paleontology is placed at the junction of the earth sciences, biological sciences, and even the human sciences if we take into account human paleontology. It has made important contributions to all of our modern notions of the growth dynamics of our planet, the diversification of life, and the advent of humanity.

Without a proper knowledge of fossils, it would have been almost impossible to specify the order in which geological beds were deposited over the globe (chronostratigraphy), or to establish the geological correlations between neighboring regions or continents. Our scale of calculating the relative geologic time of eras, periods, stages, and geological horizons depends almost entirely on fossil analysis; it was gradually developed by paleontologists from all nations and can be used in any sector of the globe. Fossil study plays a part in prospecting most sedimentary beds, and often in developing plans for their exploitation. This is especially true in the case of coal and oil sites, but also for beds filled with oolitic iron of bio-physico-chemical origin, for some beds of usable grades of copper, lead, vanadium, and uranium, and for numerous metallic minerals associated with the bio-sedimentary deposits in special paleo-environments. The identification of fossils can also be used in studies of layers of phosphates, sulphurs and sulphates, gypsum, special sands, and certain limestones and clays.

In 1912, when Alfred Wegener published his theory of continental drift, proposing that the continents had begun as a single land mass to become separated and distanced from each other, he based his theories on geophysical proofs and paleontological evidence. Geophysicians have made great use of this hypothesis in the theory of plate tectonic based, in part, on the expansion of the oceanic floor.

Paleoecology, which studies fossil species in their reciprocal relations and in relation to environments of the past, is of capital interest because of its illumination of today's equilibria: the natural environment that forms our vital framework is nothing more than the precarious endpoint or the momentary result of a series of transformations that have shaped the terrestrial world since the beginning of geological time.

The distribution of fossil populations throughout the world and during different geological periods, which we call paleobiogeography, lets us grasp the causes and origins of the current distribution of animal and plant life in different areas of the world. Thanks to paleontology, the great question of life's origins has met with responses that have aided biochemical and geochemical research undertaken in this field. The principle of life's evolution or transformationism has acquired its characteristic consistency thanks to the gradual reconstruction of fossil lines. Without these tangible proofs of life's many changing forms, it would be but a wild and unverifiable hypothesis. The classification of plants and animals by orders, genera, and species, is really the "catalogue of transformationism." Without paleontology's support showing the links between current forms through the intermediary of lines of evolution when they exist, it would have remained on a very risky level indeed.

Even the biological notion of a species, now linked to the dynamics of plant and animal populations, can draw numerous lessons from fossil examples based on precise statistical studies indicating genetic rhythms directly unobservable in nature itself. "Nature" represents no more than a moment in the evolving continuum of life. And the phenomenon of speciation (the transformation of one species into another) requires time lapses wholly disproportionate to those offered the searcher in the "living laboratory" of contemporary nature.

The many evolutionary stages revealed to the researcher by geological series have allowed paleontology to extend our knowledge of morphofunctional analysis and comparative anatomy. This is made possible through the study of the adaptive translations of organs and the mechanics of their articulation, and through the study of bone connections and the heights or gaits they permit. Thus paleontologists have been able to identify a number of relations between encephalic volume and the acquisition of vertical posture in human descendants, with all the anatomical and physical implications that result.

22

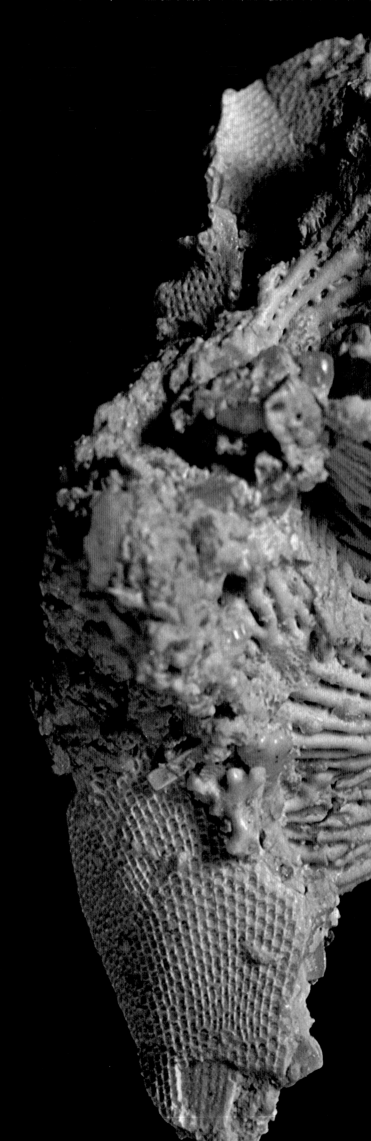

23

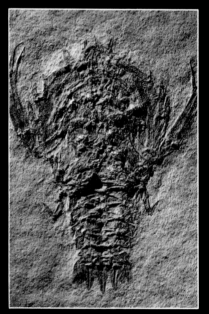

24

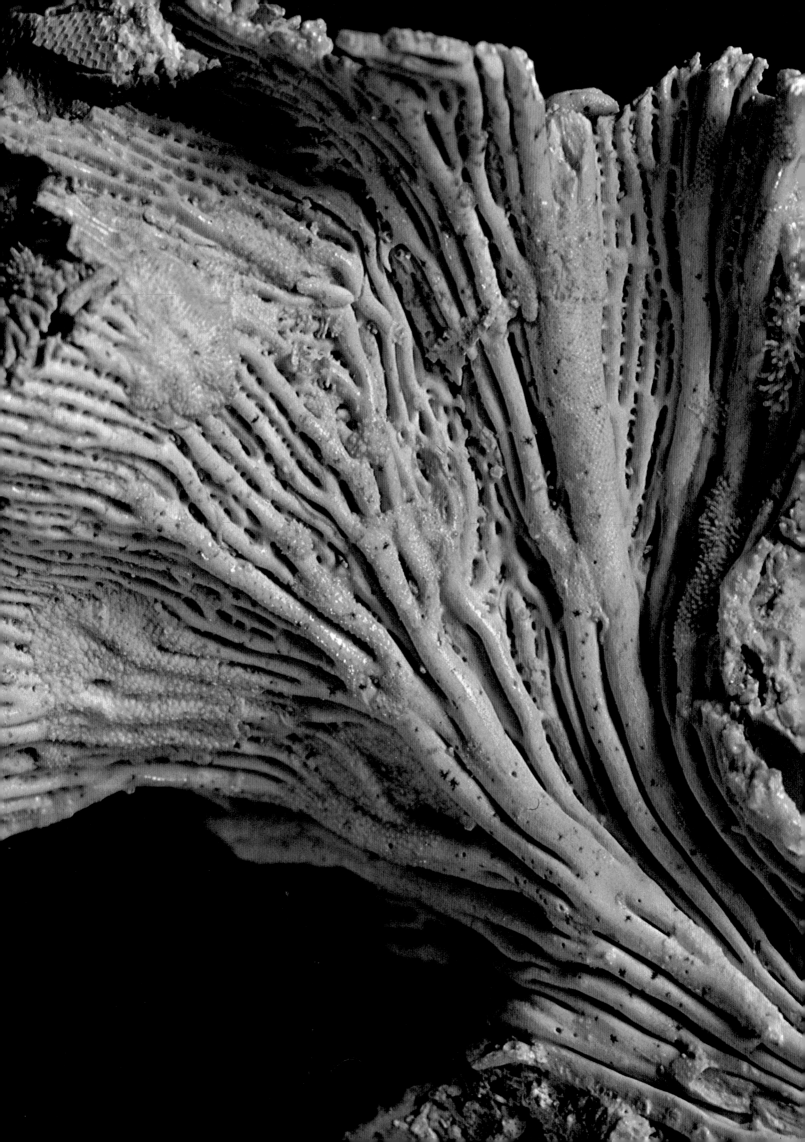

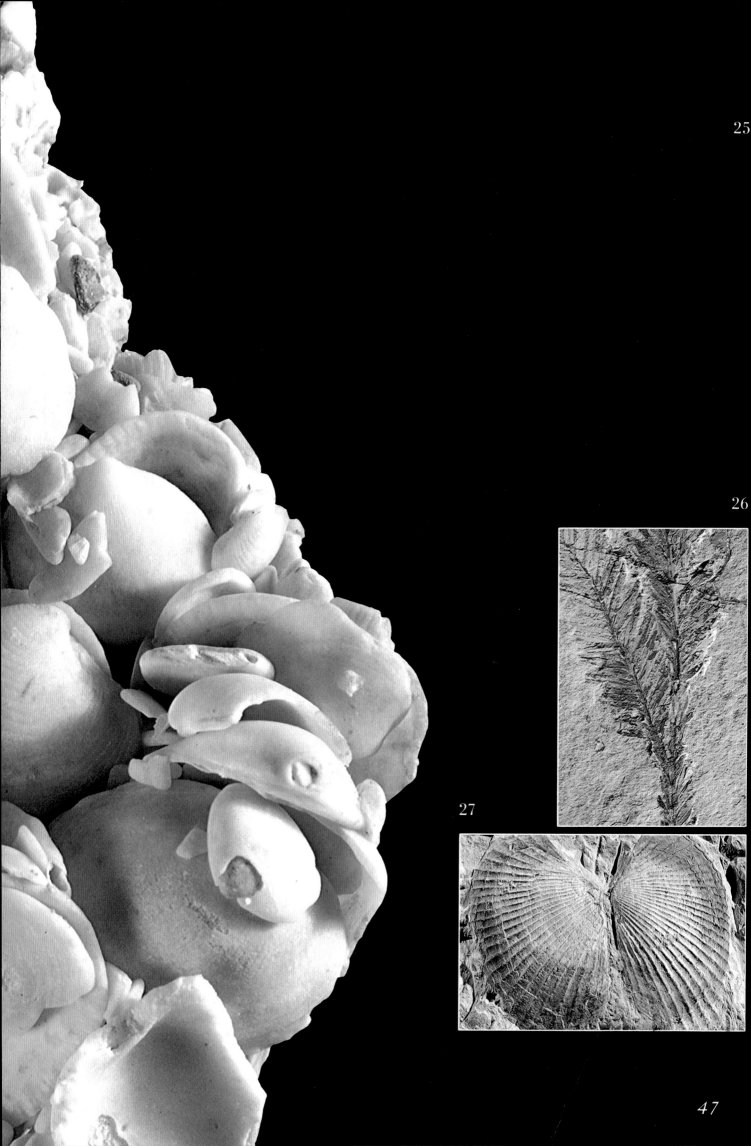

25

26

27

47

31

32

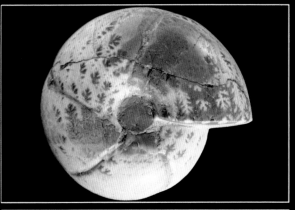

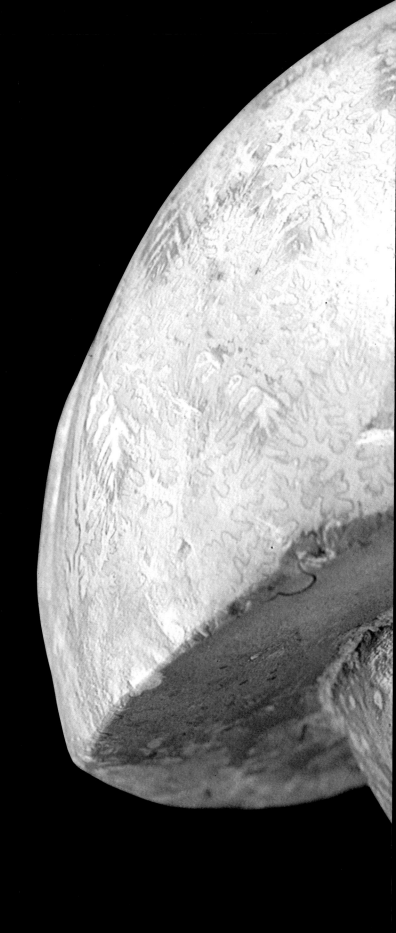

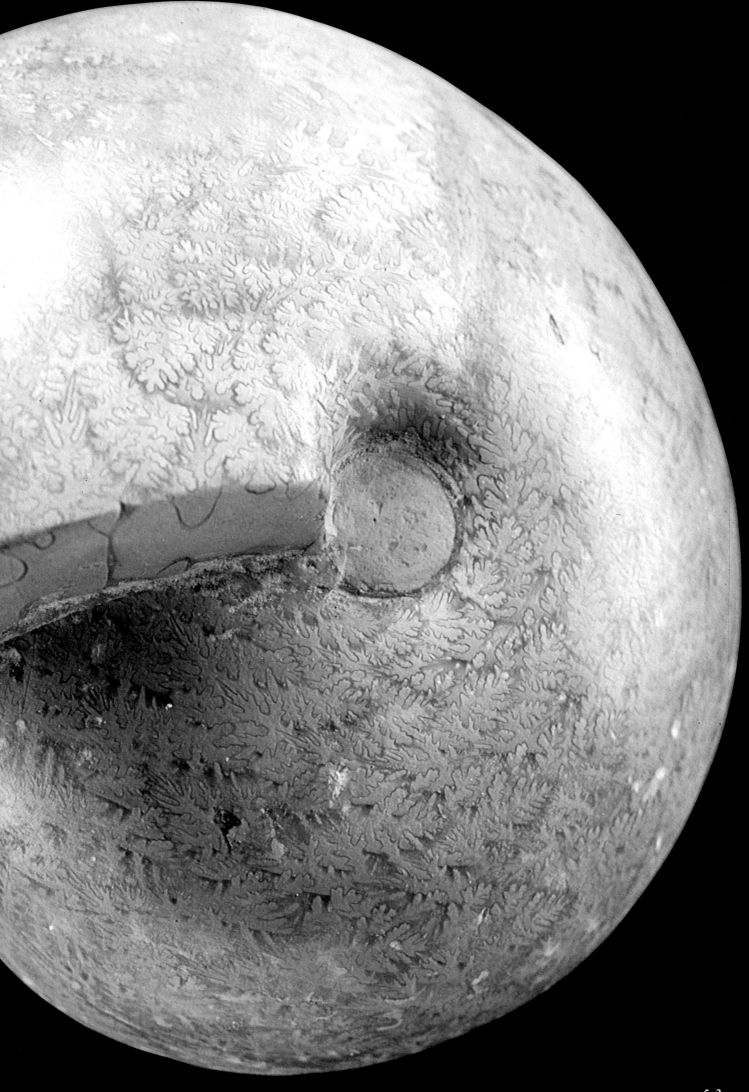

8

39

54

43

44

45
46

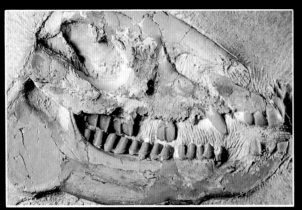

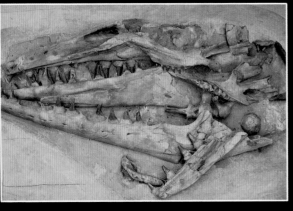

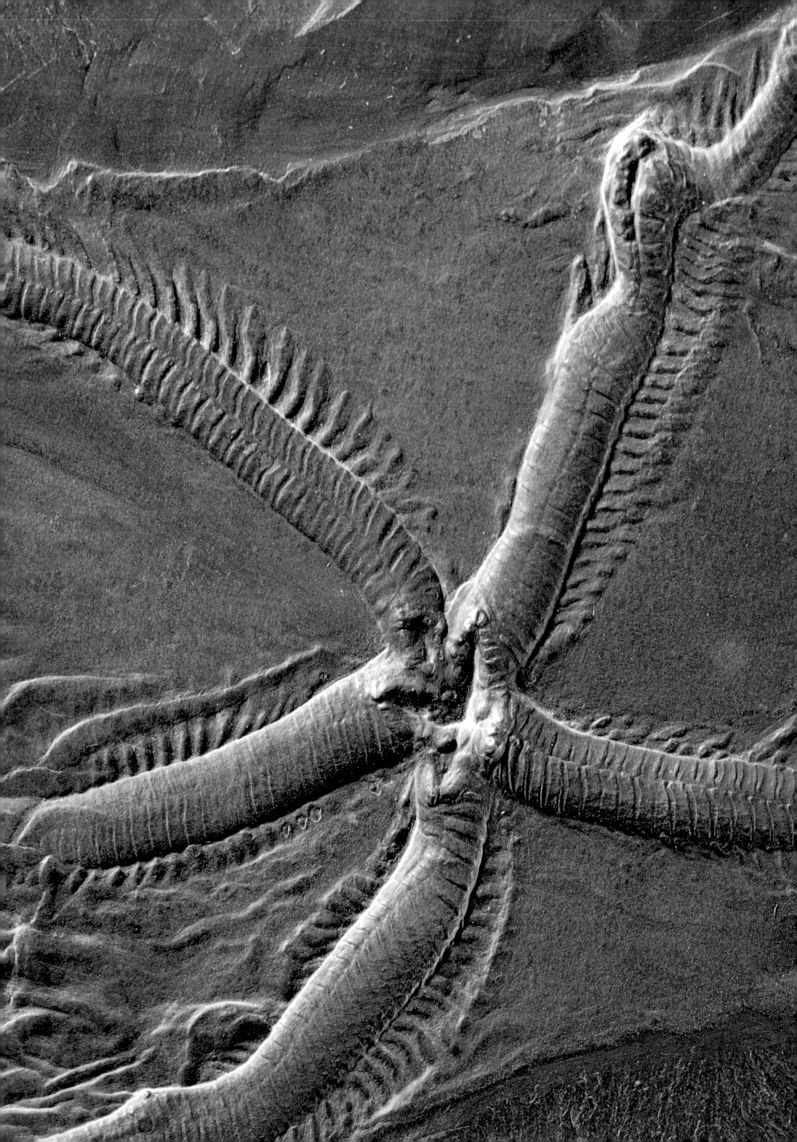

2. *Fossilization, an Exceptional Occurrence*

48

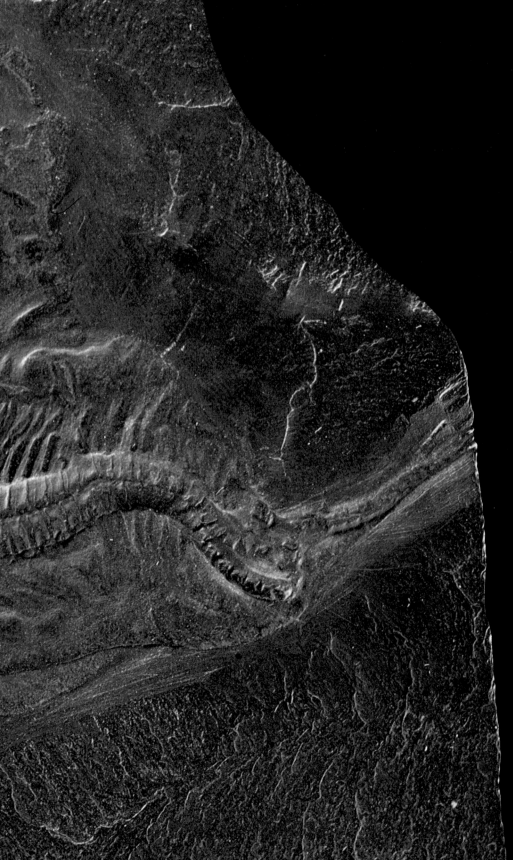

The economy of nature tolerates only a minimum of loss. As soon as an animal or plant dies, the nutritive substances comprising it are reutilized in food chains. Only when an organism is covered by a protective layer of sediment such as silt, sand, or lime soon after death can it escape total destruction. Thus, we have far more information about the ancient organisms of oceans, lakes, marshes, and waterways, with their generally mobile and rapidly sedimented bottoms, than about those that lived upon land. Deserts, however, have always provided an exception to this rule since sand can quickly cover fallen animals.

Of the innumerable species, forms, and individuals that have lived on our planet, in the past, only a few traces remain preserved from destruction. These are the fossils. And if they appear abundant and diversified in some extraordinary sites, the small fraction of the number of species we find represented in the fossil record should give us no illusions about the importance or magnitude of the initial populations. Thus fossils have an important place in the scientific and cultural heritage of all lands.

Fossilization as a Chance Event

Fossilization is the result of exceptional circumstances in which numerous factors have played a part—the actual constitution of the organism, the conditions of its death and its burial in a shifting sediment, the speed of consolidation of this sediment, the complex chemical reactions produced within it, the combined or successive actions of tectonics, metamorphism, and the washing or erosion of sediments—before a chance discovery permits man to gather the remains.

Nevertheless, when fossil structures have not been totally destroyed or denatured by dissolution, recrystallization, or metamorphosis, they can remain so fine in detail that they appear like living organisms. This is true not only of morphological structures (the morphological details of micro-organisms, the veins of leaves, the ornamentation of shells or bony sheets, or internal anatomical structures), but also of histological structures (the micro-organization of crystal in granules, fibers or flakes in plant remains, or the calcified tissues of animals). And if the oldest sediments furnish fewer fossils than more recent sediments, the organic structures are not necessarily less well preserved. Indeed, it is often quite the reverse.

49

This ophiuroid (Ophiura decheni), an echinoderm much like the starfish, is of German Devonian origin. It is a good example of fossilization in shale, a very fine ancient mud that was solidified in successive layers, then compressed by tectonics.

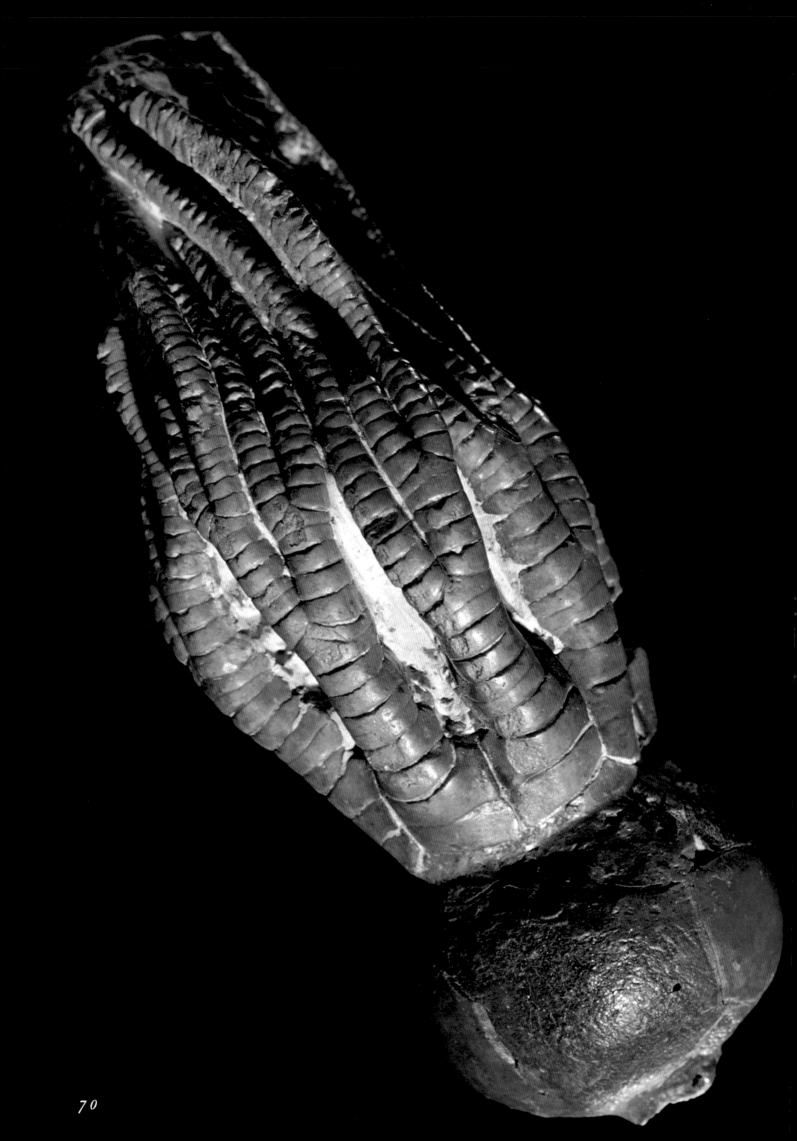

70

Argillaceous rocks (marls and limestone) generally preserve fossil structures better than chalky ones. Argillaceous sediments are laid down in silts that completely line the interstices and internal cavities of fossils before hardening and are almost impermeable—thus limiting oxidation and dissolution.

Since they are fine-grained and coherent, sandstone sediments lend themselves fairly well to the conservation of fossils. Argilo-sandstone sediments generally have been the best preservers of imprints and casts from organisms without hard parts, like jelly-fish, most larvae, and certain shell-less mollusks. Without such exceptional proofs, we could only guess at the existence of these and many other animals.

Various marine invertebrates, notably worms and arthropods, have also left marks of their presence in fossil sediments. Since the Cambrian period their paths have been marked by burrows of characteristic diameter, orientation, form, and length (burrows for eating or locomotion, or refuge), although the invertebrates themselves have not been fossilized because of their fragility.

Similarly, an inventory has been made of many imprints. Some of them belong to animals that are well known in their fossil states—tracks of trilobates from the Paleozoic era, reptile footprints (particularly of dinosaurs) from the Mesozoic, imprints of birds' steps from the Tertiary. These, in the absence of other indications, reveal their passage or migration. Most of these imprints, however, still have not been attributed to specific animals, particularly those that are the sole indications left by many invertebrates. But still we know, thanks to them, that life was flourishing in regions and epochs one might otherwise have thought deserted because they are void of fossil bodies.

These fragments, parts, or remains of organisms (casts, molds, shells, carapaces, bones) are not the only proofs of life to come to us from the depths of geological time. We can also identify "biosedimentary indications," testifying to the organisms' presence or physiological activity, or to the manifestations or effects by which they have marked their "environments."

In the complex scale of organic sediments, we can first cite carbons, lignites, bituminous coals, and oils as revealers of biological activity, although their constituting organisms (plants and micro-organisms) can generally no longer be identified. Amber, which is nothing more than a fossil resin, indicates the development of immense resinaceous forests

50

Apiocrinus magnificus, Upper Jurassic echinoderm from Charentes, France. Finding fossil crinoids still retaining stalks and arms is a rare event. Here the stalk has disappeared, but the crown is equipped with all its arms.

in different epochs and eras. Spores and pollens, grains, fruits, eggs, and nests, which are lodged in sediments in varying degrees of abundance, reveal the presence or proximity of a variety of types of organisms.

Sometimes the abundance of fossil vertebrate groups is disclosed by excremental masses called coproliths. Famous layers of these are known, such as one from Gloucester, England, which is thought to have belonged to the dinosaur family. Certain limestones of marine origin are similarly composed of "pellets" formed from the digestion of silts by various organisms (larvae, mollusks, crustaceans). Other organisms have left traces of incrustation, or have revealed the type of support they were fixed in. Oysters' adhesive surfaces indicate whether they colonized wooden supports, rocky surfaces, or other shells.

A thorough examination of many plant and mineral fossils shows the varied marks of parasitism. Other fossils present traces of physiological traumas, revealing frequent accidents that tell us much about their lives. Traces of predation are equally present—pierced or broken mollusk shells (often indicating specific predators), sectioned fish, the crushed bones of reptiles or mammals. All these indications bring us information about the way of life and environment of fossil species.

51

Pilosisporites, *a rare and remarkable fern spore from the Cretaceous soils of Israel, measures no more than 40 microns. Fossilization has preserved its decoration of vegetable chitin, shown in its smallest details by this photograph taken with an electronic scanning microscope.*

Material Transformations

All organic substances undergo constant transformations throughout time. The speed and complexity of transformation varies according to the nature of the organism, to biochemical reactions, and to the lithological, geochemical, and mechanical processes undergone by the surrounding sediments.

Vegetable materials, beyond their transformation into peat, brown coal, and carbon, usually leave only simple carbonic imprints since they are isolated in rocks. Yet, under certain conditions they may be transformed into calcite or silica (chalcedony, jasper, or opal).

Only calcified or silicate elements (the worn forms of micro-organisms, coral skeletons, crustacean carapaces, bones, vertebral shells, and teeth) are left behind as animal remains. The calcified elements can be found preserved in the original insulating materials without important transformation. But after the sediment hardens they are frequently dissolved and replaced by crystalline calcite or by substances such as sulphurs of iron or copper (pyrites, marcasites), hematite, gypsum, silica (chalcedony, jasper, opal), or bituminous coal. If no other material is substituted after the carbonate or phosphate in the original lime disintegrates, a cavity is left within the rock. We call this cavity, which accurately measures the fossil's volume, an imprint or cast. An exact replica can be constructed by filling the cavity with a plastic solution or resin, thus artificially completing the process of natural substitution.

Fossil Colors

The fossil world is often thought to be colorless. This notion is incorrect, although the colors tinting fossils usually are not those of the original pigments, but rather those of the varied oxides that have saturated them during the course of fossilization. The most widespread oxides in nature are oxides of iron (ferrous and ferric oxides), copper, and manganese. This is why fossil colors, like the encasing sedimentary rocks, are usually tones of ochre, blue, or green, sometimes red or blood-colored, simply white like limestone, or black in the case of vegetable matter transformed into carbon.

And yet under exceptional circumstances, some mollusk shells still show the marks of their original coloration. We see this in the shells of various bivalves and gastropods, some of which date from the Carboniferous period (300 million years ago) and show color patterns of longitudinal or transversal bands, broken or sinuous lines, and geometrically placed spots. Even if these traces of pigmentation are obvious, the colors themselves are still distorted, since they are always in the ochre tones characteristic of the oxides that have acted on them throughout the course of fossilization.

Fossils "In Flesh and Bone"

Since bacterial and chemical agents quickly attack them, soft tissues are usually eliminated long before fossilization can occur. But the rare exceptions to this rule are the most remarkable.

Dinoflagellates, micro-organisms of cellulose tissue, are found preserved as organic material in many flints from the Craie. The myriad insects and organisms trapped in fossil resins (amber) tens of millions of years ago are as well preserved today as if they had been purposely sheltered from destruction in plastic. Numerous specimens of the mammoth and woolly rhinocerous, moreover, have been frozen in the Siberian ice for millenia and count among the rare vertebrates to reach us "in flesh and bone," with skin and fleece intact. According to travelers' tales, the flesh was fresh enough to be eaten by dogs and probably even by several indigenous Turanians.

Natural oil lakes of various geological periods (notably in North America) have similarly permitted the perfect preservation of millions of organisms. Some of these are heavy terrestrial vertebrates (reptiles from the Mesozoic period, mammals from the Tertiary and Quaternary) that became mired in the oil and are now found "mummified" in asphalt.

The Great Paleontological Expeditions

The Nineteenth Century

The naturalists of the first large scientific explorations in the nineteenth century aimed at a systematic harvest of all interesting items, whether animal, vegetable, or mineral. Among these, fossils held a prominent place. One of the most famous expeditions was a South American voyage by Alcide d'Orbigny, which took no less than 7 years (from 1826 to 1833). D'Orbigny made an extraordinary collection of observations ranging from ethnology to geology, and brought back quantities of material—including important fossils—from all fields of the natural sciences. This was the first large paleontological collection from South America. It found a place in the Museum of Natural History in Paris, where d'Orbigny was to hold the first chair in paleontology.

In succeeding years, scientific expeditions became increasingly specialized. Since then, innumerable prospecting campaigns or digs have

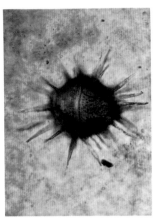

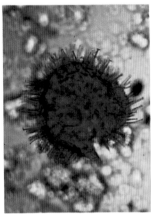

52, 53

Operculidium, *from the Australian Miocene, and* Hystrichosphaeridium, *from the Quaternary period in France. These two dinoflagellates, here much enlarged and artificially colored, owe their marvelous preservation to the fact that they were often trapped alive in colloidal silica, which saved from destruction even their most delicate cellulosic horns.*

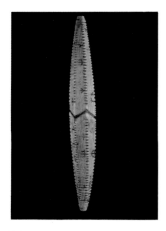

54

Long before real expeditions in search of mammoths were organized, mammoth tusks were greatly sought after for trade. Fossil ivory has been exploited since antiquity. This primitive Orthodox calendar was carved from mammoth ivory by the Asian Yakuts.

been organized, with results enriching the many paleontological collections developing throughout the world. No matter how distant or how fruitful, these missions were always captivating and usually required a minimum of organization. But collecting certain fossils can require thorough expeditions, armed with specialized tools and involving lengthy preparations.

One of the first large paleontological expeditions took place in 1901, after a mammoth was found frozen in the ice of Berezoka in Oriental Siberia. It was organized by the St. Petersburg Academy of Sciences under the direction of Otto Herz. After reaching Irkoutsk on May 14th, the expedition traveled by horse or sleigh for more than 2000 kilometers before reaching the site on September 2nd, almost four months later. The mammoth was then dismembered, dissected, and loaded on sleds which carried it back to Irkoutsk; then it was shipped by railway to St. Petersburg. Since that time its skeleton has been exhibited in the Zoological Museum of St. Petersburg (now Leningrad).

Later, other Siberian expeditions brought back the fossil remains of various species (mammoths, woolly rhinoceri, wild oxen, sea elephants, and deer) that are of considerable interest to science. In 1949, the Academy of Leningrad asked Professor E. N. Pavlovsky to direct an expedition to the peninsula of Taïmyr, on the banks of the glacial Arctic, to bring back a remarkable mammoth specimen partially freed from the ice and threatened with decomposition.

Less perilous was the "dinosaur hunt" undertaken by American researchers under Professors Marsh and Cope. It began in 1868 and ultimately led to a collection of wholly remarkable pieces. In 1903, Professor Osborn extracted the twenty-two-meter-long skeleton of a brontosaurus (the giant of dinosaurs) from the Upper Jurassic sediments of Como Bluff, Wyoming. Today it completely dominates the main gallery of the American Museum of Natural History, though surrounded by numerous other striking reconstructions.

The Twentieth Century

Encouraged by the American public's enthusiasm, such excavations multiplied throughout the United States while the strata containing dinosaurs were also being prospected in Europe, Africa, and Asia. In 1915, the federal government of the United States decided to maintain the remarkable "Morrison beds" in Utah, where visitors can now admire numerous dinosaur skeletons *in situ,* just as they exist in the sediments.

In 1924 Professor Dart discovered the first Australopithecan cranium, estimated to be approximately 2,500,000 years old, near Botswana, South Africa. Following that discovery, paleontologists launched a study of the traces of primitive humanity and found one after another in Africa, Europe, China, and Indonesia. The famous beds of the Omo valley in Ethiopia were discovered at the beginning of the century by French voyagers and delivered the oldest known remains of Australopithecus. A mission was organized from 1932 to 1933 by the National Museum of Natural History in Paris, under the direction of Professor Arambourg. The interest of the findings impelled a second expedition of French, Kenyan, and American teams whose excavating campaigns followed each other in succession starting in 1967. These digs gradually stretched to the banks of Lake Rodolphe, then to the basin of Lake Baringo, Kenya, with the entry of an English team, and finally into the Awash valley, Ethiopia, bringing enormous discoveries on the anatomy, living conditions, way of life, and distribution of these 1.5- to 3-million-year-old hominoids.

In 1968, following the paleontological missions launched by English, Swedish, and Danish teams in the great North (especially Greenland and Spitsberg), the French National Center for Scientific Research (CNRS) decided to mount an important expedition to Spitsberg, armed with an ice-breaking boat and two helicopters. Under the direction of Professor J. P. Lehman, twenty searchers from the National Museum of History and the Universities of Montpellier and Poitiers left Le Havre on June 25, 1969, to return two and a half months later with 23 tons of fossils. Notable among the specimens were extraordinary plants from the Devonian, Triassic, and Tertiary periods, some agnaths (armored "fish" without jaws) from Devonian and Silurian times, as well as numerous Triassic vertebrates such as coelacanths and stegocephaloids. These findings, which today are being studied at the Institute of Paleontology of the Museum (Paris), have enlarged the 60 tons of paleontological material brought back from various African missions by researchers from this institute and are quite as remarkable for the methods of collection employed.

These varying types of missions require of paleontologists a

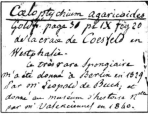

55

Great digging explorations are not all that fed the world's paleontological collections. Generous collectors have contributed remarkable pieces, like this Coeloptychium agaricoides, *a sponge from the Upper Cretaceous in Westphalia.*

wide breadth of knowledge, solid technical abilities, organization, and strong physical prowess. Nature, whether fossil or living, must be primarily observed in the field, and paleontologists, like other specialists of the earth and life sciences, must be men of the field as well as of the laboratory.

Industrial and Decorative Exploitation of Fossils

56

Common chalk, photographed by electronic microscope, reveals an unbelievable accumulation of coccoliths, limestone algae that are complex in structure but so small that a cubic millimeter contains 10 million of them. Here we have Gartenerago confussus, *a coccolith from the chalk of the Paris basin.*

Coals, lignites, peat, tar, oil, and natural gases, originating as organic fossil material and forming throughout time, are actually solar energy transformed by photosynthesis into matter and stored by entrapment in the subsoil. This is the fossil energy that, with all its derivatives, allows our technologically advanced societies to appreciate the benefits of growth. But these are not the only useful substances that industry draws from the fossil world.

The great layers of phosphate are nothing more than masses of fish and mammal carcasses or bird excrement in which salts of phosphoric acid have become concentrated during the course of fossilization. The phosphorites of Quercy (now depleted for many years) and Florida, the phosphate-filled sands of the Ardennes and the Meuse, and the marls and phosphated calcites of North Africa furnish several examples. Their importance in fabricating superphosphates ranks them among the greatest riches of the subsoil. Peru and Chile contain important deposits of nitrates of soda, which are exploited under the name of Chilean saltpeter and are fossil masses of organic nitrogenous materials transformed by the fermentation of microbes.

Diatomites, very hard, fine, porous flinty rocks formed of diatom frustules (in the ratio of 1,500 million individuals to cubic centimeter), serve many ends: because they are light (density 0.2), they were used for building the dome of Santa Sophia at Constantinople; they are excellent thermal and noise insulators and are used to make special filters. Since they can absorb eight times their weight in water, they form the absorbing support of nitroglycerine in dynamite; under the name *tripoli*, or fossil meal, they are used for polishing metals and scouring tubs.

Radiolarites—black, grey, or red flinty rocks that are very hard and beautifully polished—are composed through the accumulation of radiolaria, micro-organisms that first appeared in the Precambrian era. They are often used in making jewelry today. White chalk, used for many purposes (limestone, whitewash and tempera painting, scouring pastes known as Spanish or Meudon white, tracing sticks, chalk water), is mostly formed of microscopic debris of coccolithoporids and foraminifera deposited at the bottom of Cretaceous seas.

Limestones, principally used for cement blocks, construction materials, paving roads, or improving agricultural fields, are sediments of basically organogenic origin. They were formed by accumulations of marine shells (nummulitic limestones, shelly limestones, faluns, rudist limestones, coral limestones) by biophysicochemical precipitation (oolitic limestones), by the effects of networks of microscopic algae (travertine and soft-water tuffs, stromatolithic limestones), or by a combination of these three principle processes (gravelly limestones, pisolite or pseudo-oolitic limestones, limestones with algae). Some very fine and compact limestones can be used in place of marble (travertine, limestone from Comblanchien). Metamorphosed, they fall into the actual category of marbles, which owe their beauty to the form or color of the fossils they enclose and are sought for special decorative effects.

Fossil ivory stimulated a lively trade. This trade began in the ninth and tenth centuries with the discovery of important mammoth sites in Siberia and has built the reputations of markets in Iakoutsk and Irkutsk. To this day, it is still pursued, despite the fairly low commercial value of ivory. Yellow amber or succin, a fossil resin found on the shores of the Baltic Sea and in Sicily, has been used since the Bronze Age for necklaces and pendants. And fossils themselves are the object of an active trade, which is international in scope and frequently illegal.

Fossils and Artistic Expression

Representations of Fossils

A desire to represent as well as describe objects of curiosity and study is continually demonstrated throughout history. The first works on

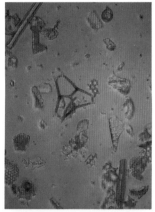

57, 58

Diatom and radiolarians, rocks exploited for their hardness, are basically formed of siliceous micro-organisms. Here we see enlarged and artificially colored specimens of a Corbisema *(triangular silicoflagellate) and a diatom from a tripoli of the Cretaceous period in the Urals. Below are radiolaria found in Barbados.*

59

The many fragments of crinoid stems, formed of pure calcite crystals, give this marble stone its beauty and decorative value.

60, 61, 62

Though at first sought for its magical properties, amber—easy to cut and polish—has gradually become the equal of the finest precious stones. Here, a modern medallion and two small eighteenth-century Chinese sculptures.

the natural sciences were catalogues of the great sixteenth-century collections, in which artistic display plays the major role. These contain the first known representations of fossils, and clearly fidelity of representation was equated with comprehension of the object. If these first attempts appear today as naive or maladept, they are still witnesses to a new vision of a practically unknown universe.

The first engravings of fossils are often roughly made and allow only the most summary reproductions of objects. But technique became more refined during the seventeenth century. Suddenly, much—in fact everything—was artistically represented. This is the period of "figured stones" and fanciful forms, often fantastic in cast, placed beside perfectly clear animal and plant representations. In the eighteenth century, representation became remarkably precise. The engravings of the period are true works of art, finely executed and designed with great thought. Often a number of artists collaborated on the illustration of the same work. In the nineteenth century the techniques themselves were expanded. Lithography was added to drypoint and etching. Watercolor often enhanced line, particularly in plant representations. Naturalistic illustration became sumptuous, and the beautiful plates of these old books are still sought after today.

But as didactic concerns took the upper hand, illustration increasingly lost its artistic aspect to become no more than description. Lithography predominated, allowing reproduction of the modeling of forms and the details of their structures. The discovery of photography was finally to put an end to the artistic reign of scientific engraving. Modern technical developments have made photography, in its turn, capable of expressing the beauties of the fossil world.

We must rely to a large degree on imagination for reconstruction of prehistoric animals. But for a reconstruction to be useful, it must begin with a solid knowledge of the skeletal form, taking into account the junctures of muscles, the animal's bearing, and so on. This job requires the collaboration of paleontologists, anatomists, and artists. Such reconstructions, moreover, fulfill a wide variety of decorative, didactic, educational, and publicity purposes. Here we can cite the "life-size" dinosaur statues in several American parks, the work of the American painter C. R. Knight, and the fine illustrations by the Czechoslovakian artist Z. Burian. The cinema of this science-fiction era has also made use of these reconstructions and has given us the dinosaur battles in *King Kong* and Walt

Disney's adaptation of Stravinsky's *Rites of Spring,* among others.

But prehistoric art had already portrayed man's familiar animals, now largely extinct. Cave paintings depict bisons, wild horses, reindeer, mammoths, and woolly rhinoceri, which are especially notable in the caves of Font-de-Gaume, Combarelles, and Lascaux in Dordogne, as well as at Altamira in the Austrian region. Prehistoric sculpture has given us several fine ivories, and the engraving is no less intriguing: it reproduces reindeer, mammoth, bison, and bear on wood, stone, ivory, and bone. Fossil matter itself has been used as a material for our first human artifacts. We know of South Algerian arrowheads carved in the fossil wood of araucaria.

Ornamental Uses of Fossil Material

Man has employed many fossil materials for ornament and amusement. Paleolithic tombs often contain fossil mollusks, as in the Grimaldi burial grounds where skeletons were swathed in tight layers of *Nassa neritea,* interpreted as the remains of netting and loincloth. Small fossil sea urchins mounted in necklaces are documented in a Neolithic tomb; there are also instances of necklaces made from mountain bear's teeth and pierced trilobite pendants. Early men similarly used fossils for ornamental pieces or bibelots. To this day, fossil sea urchins are worn as pendants in Africa. Fragments of polished jasper and small limestone shells in an array of colors are also fashioned into necklaces, and small pyritous ammonites have always enjoyed a certain vogue in jewelry.

Amber is the most celebrated fossil substance used for ornament. From antiquity to our days, whether rough or finely worked, in a folklore or sophisticated style, amber has been as much sought after as the finest of precious stones.

Another valued jeweler's material is jet, which was extremely fashionable in the nineteenth and early twentieth centuries. The Indians of Venezuela used fragments of jet or lignite for simple ornaments. Several of these sculpted pieces are probably Precolumbian in origin.

Mammoth ivory has been crafted throughout man's history. The Arabs and the peoples of Arctic Asia used it to carve jewels, figurines, and toilet articles. Another fine example is a throne sculpted of mammoth

63, 64, 65

Fossil plants have always been choice subjects for illustrative works. Among the many richly illustrated books, Stenberg's Flora of the Primitive World, *which was published in 1838 in Prague, counts among the most remarkable, both for its abundant documentation and the beauty and accuracy of the drawings.*

ivory, which belonged to a Tartar Khan.

Less well known is the symbolic use of fossils for heraldic emblems. The city of Whitby in England, whose abbess, St. Hilda, was said to have transformed snakes into stone, has three ammonites in the form of serpents' heads in its coat-of-arms. The arms of the city of Scunthorpe and those of Dudley display two Gryphins, a trilobite of the genus *Calymene*.

Usually known as a minor art, stamp collecting is also representative of fossils' artistic appeal. Fossil vertebrates hold a major place in naturalistic representations. Though rarer, invertebrates like ammonites, trilobites, and sea urchins have also inspired engravers.

This rapid "world tour" can help us grasp the richness and originality of the artistic fields in which fossils have been a source of inspiration.

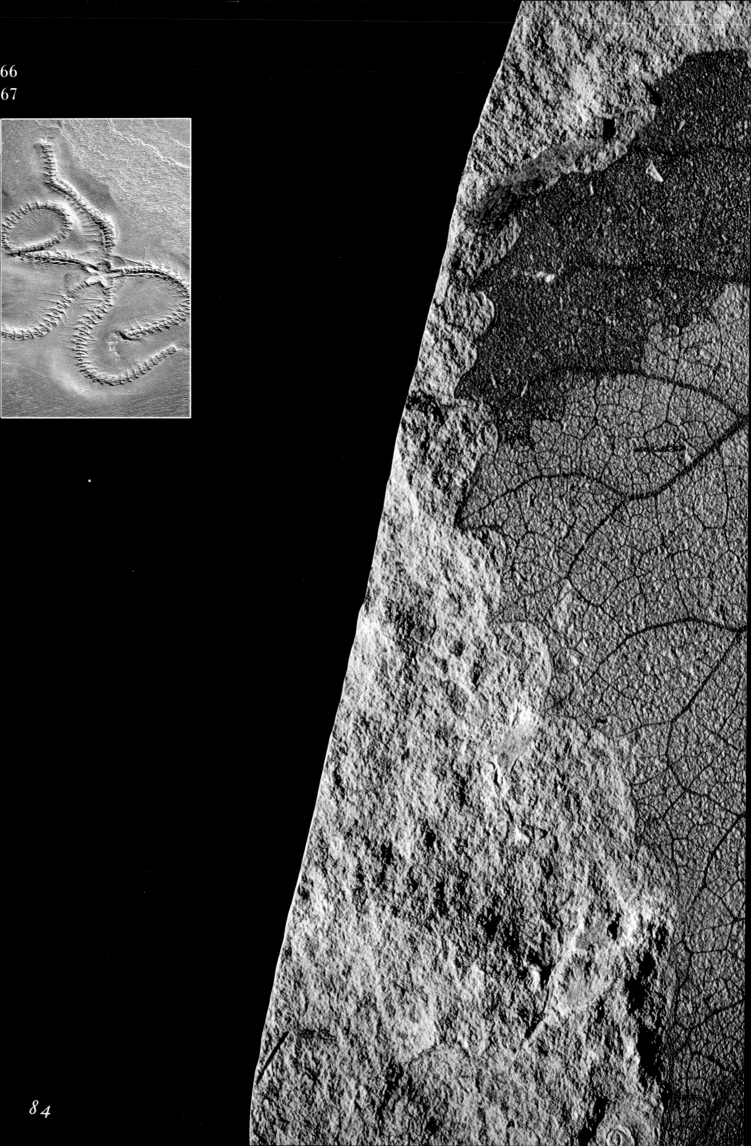

68

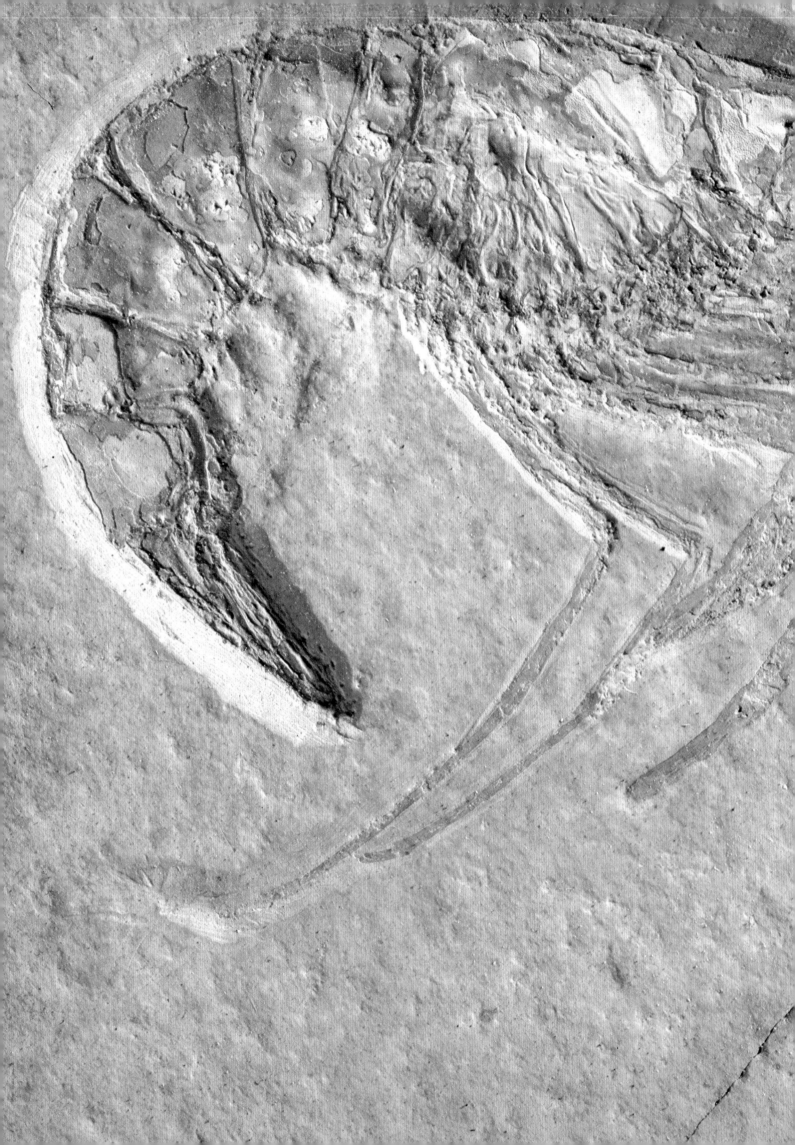

70

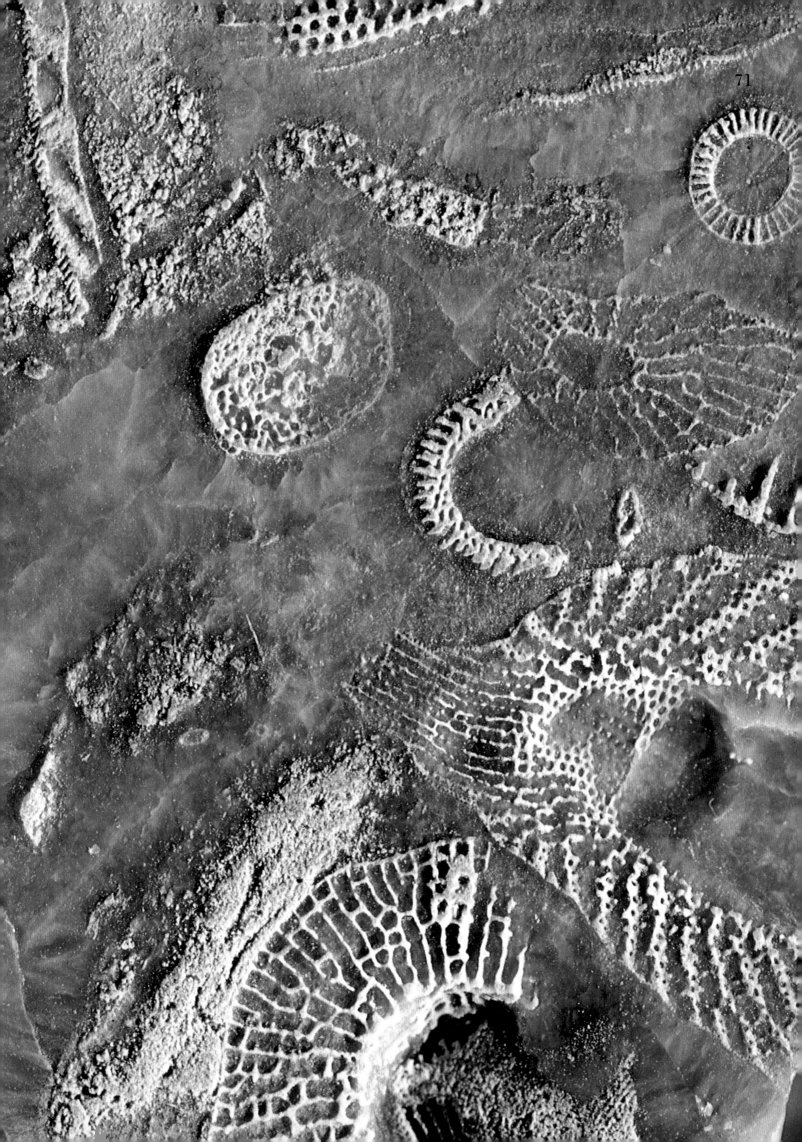

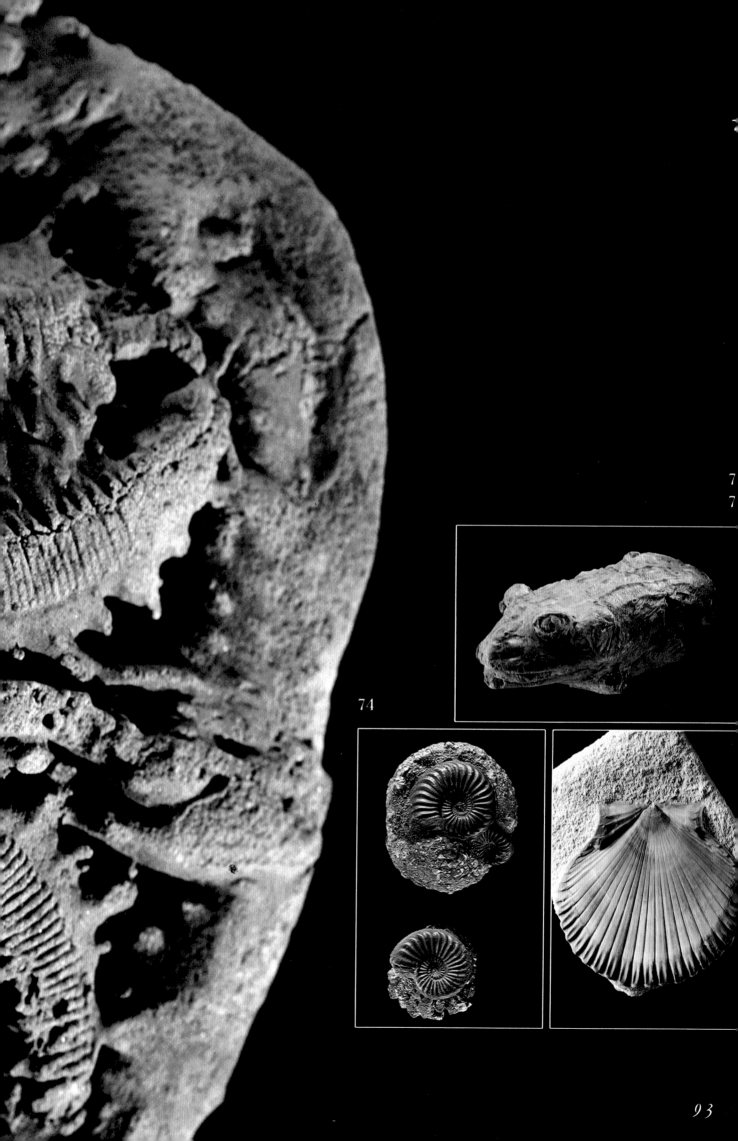

74

93

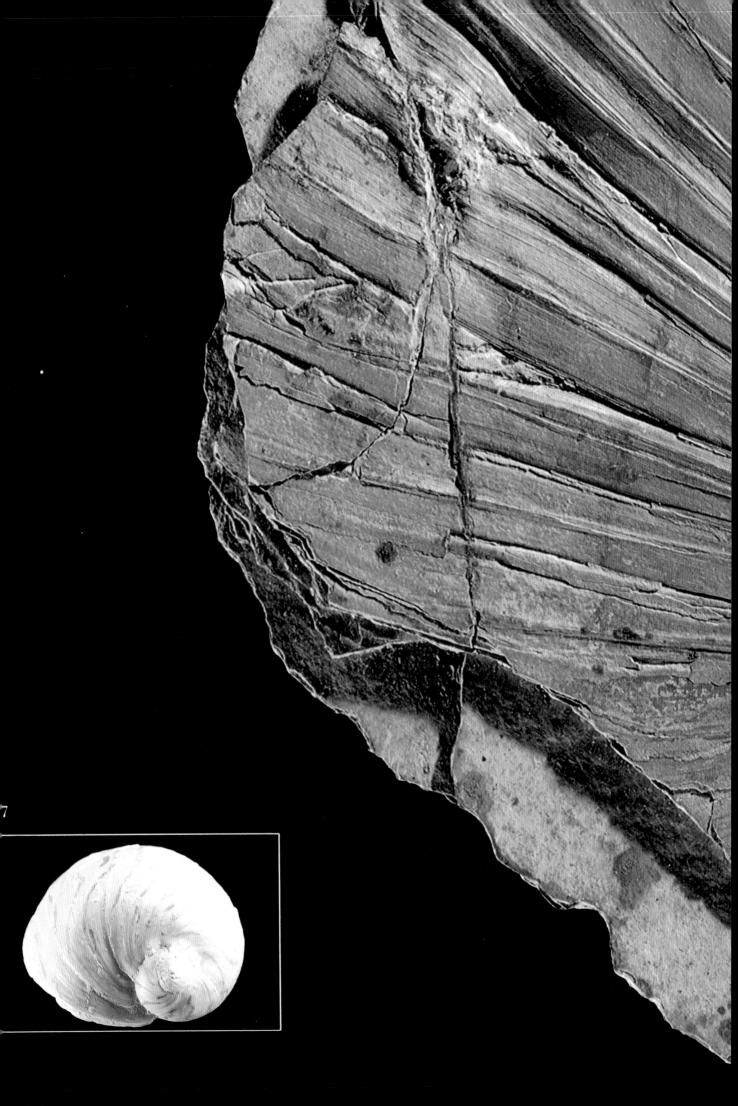

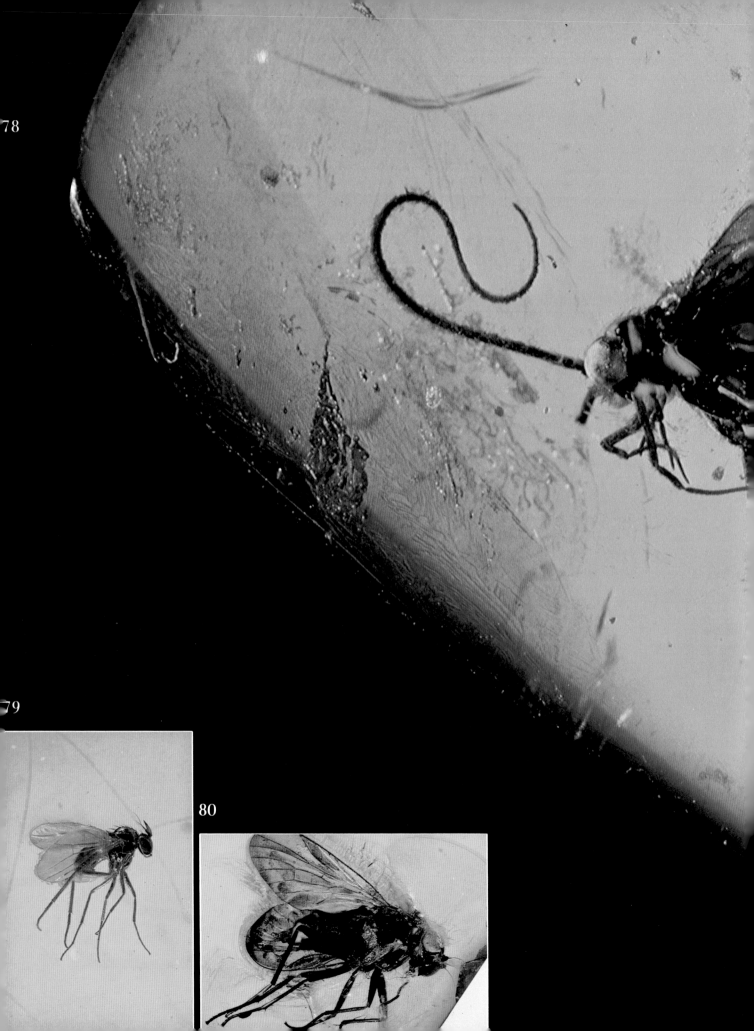

78

79

80

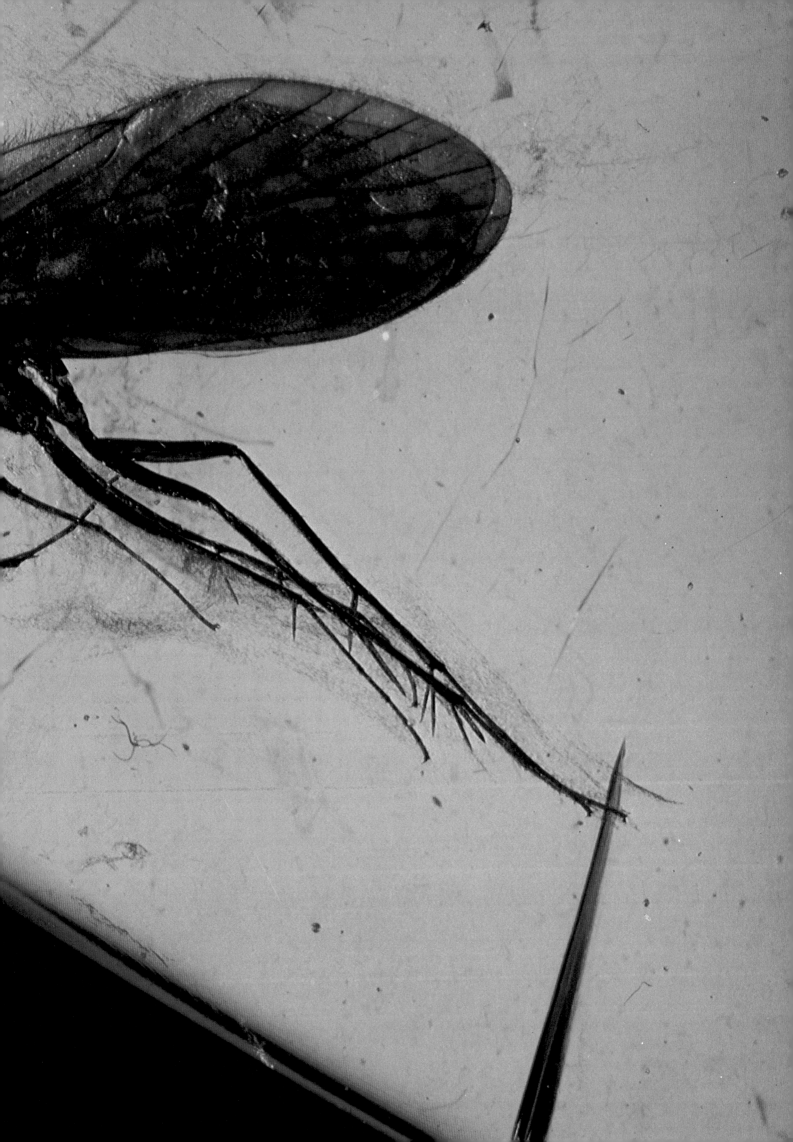

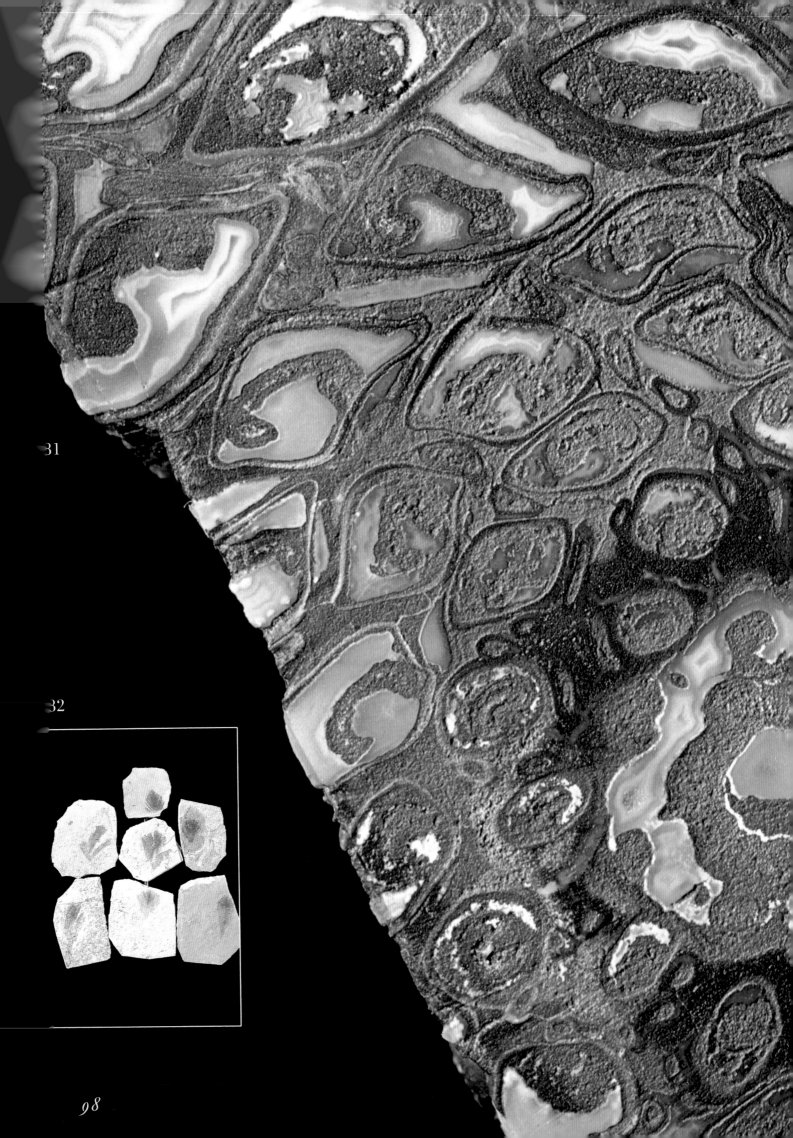

31

32

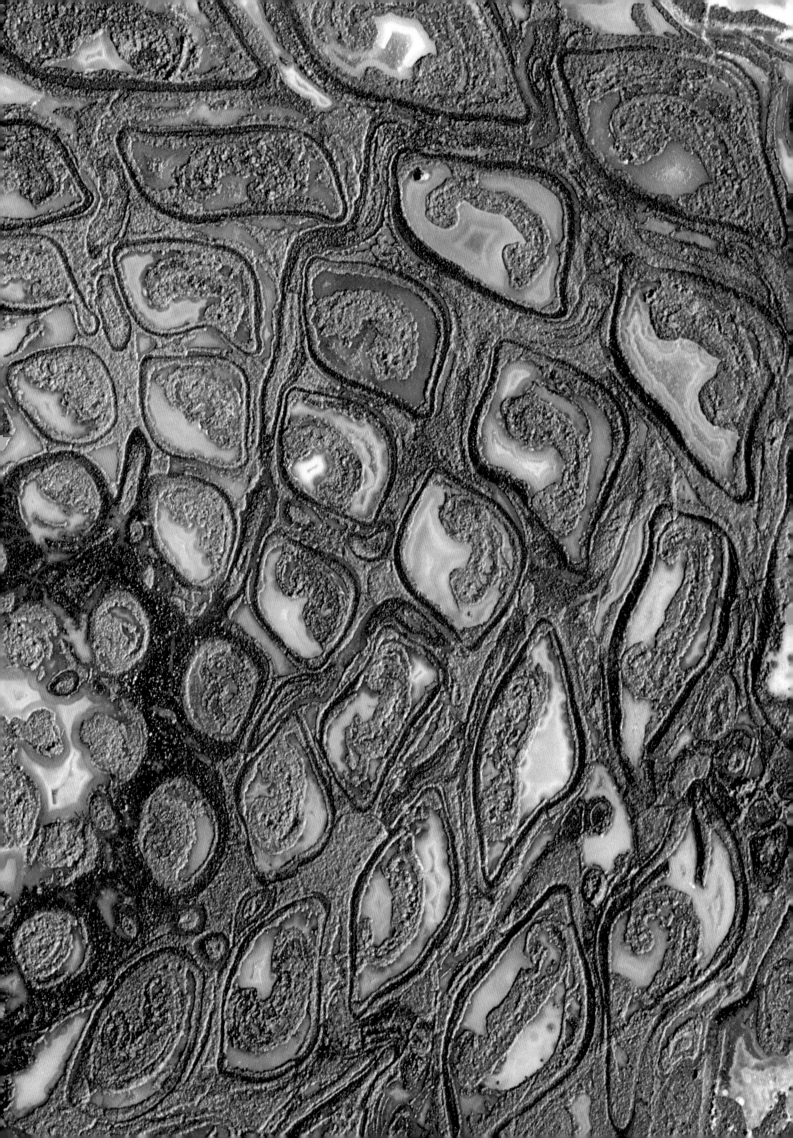

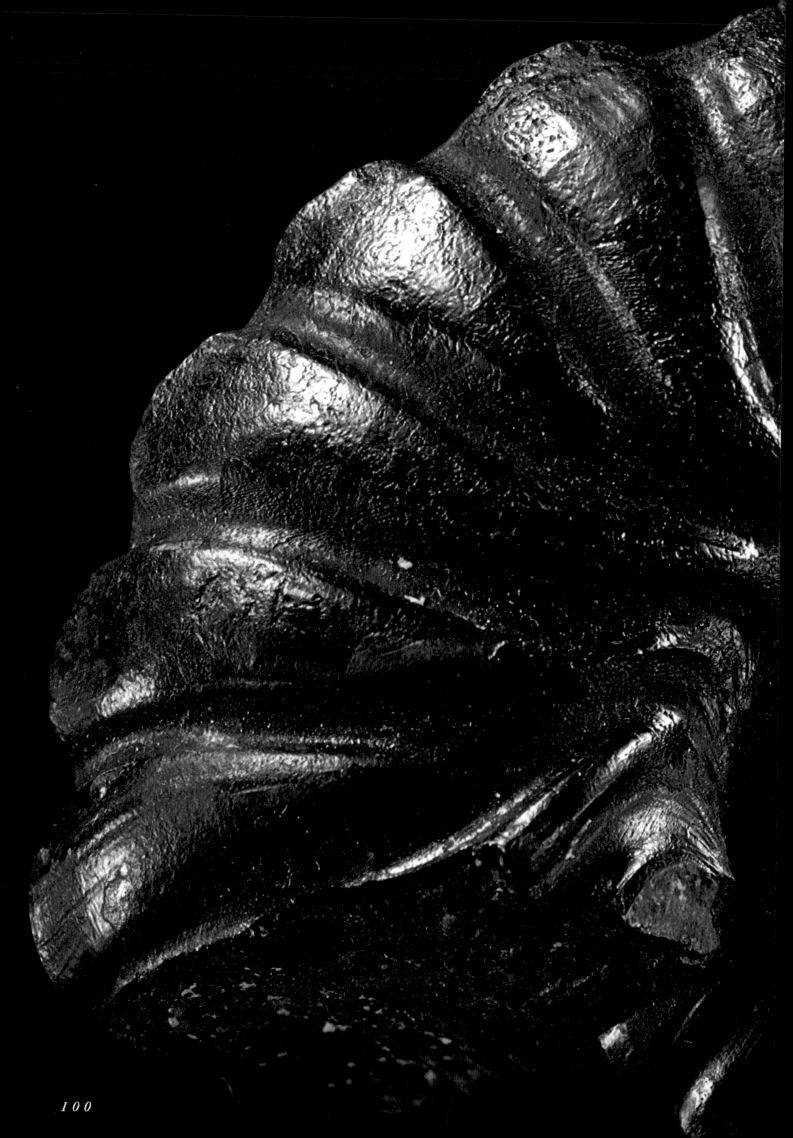

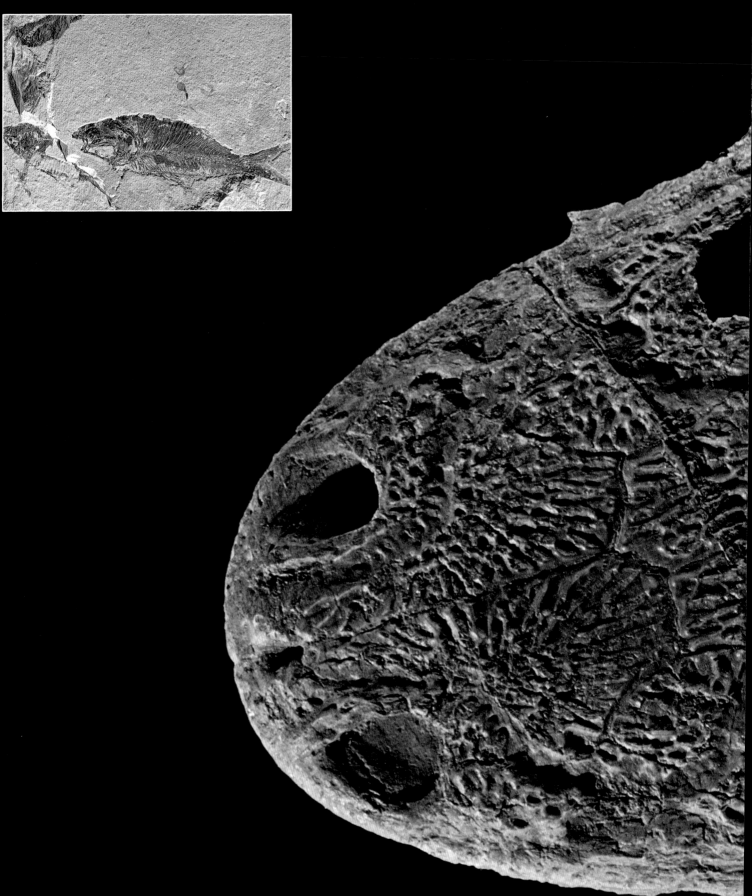

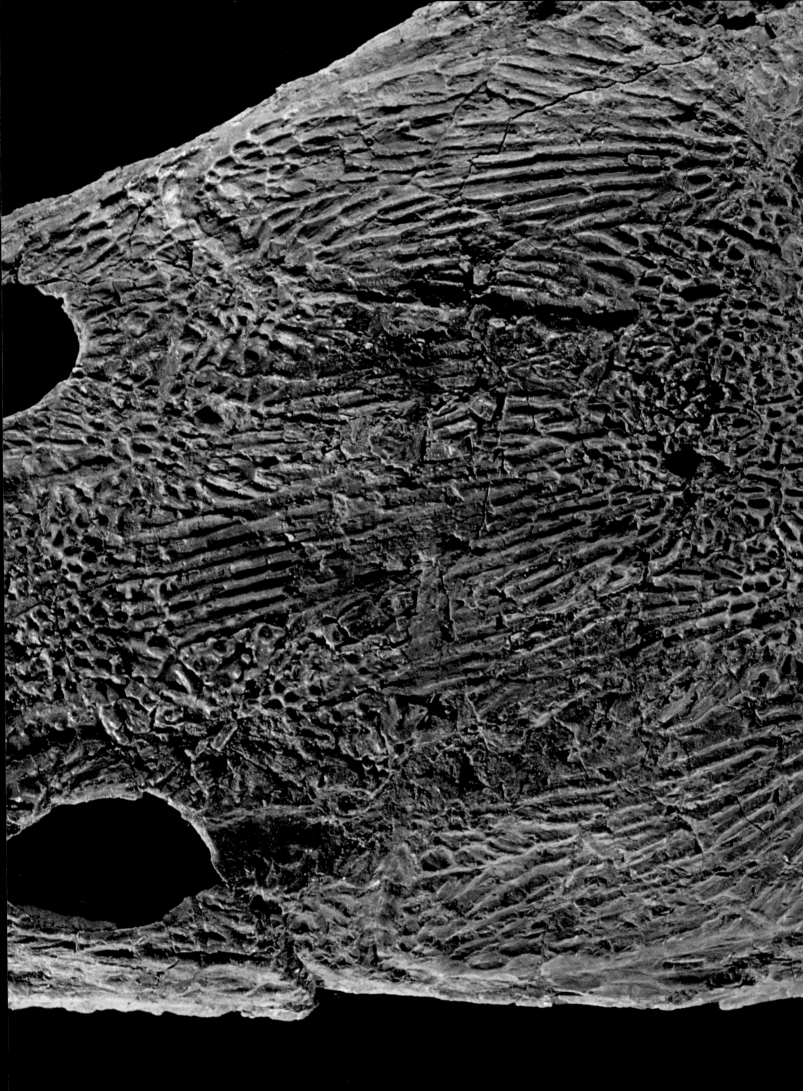

3. Richness and Strangeness of the Forms of Life

86

For two centuries, since the time of Linnaeus and the systematic inventory of the plants and animals of the world, we have remained stunned by the countless numbers of biological species, by their extraordinary diversity of forms, and by the complexity of combinations and adaptations they reveal. In the animal kingdom alone, the number of fossil and living species can be estimated at several million, and we are constantly finding new ones that had formerly eluded the investigator's eye. If we make a comparative examination of this fantastic biological diversity, we are tempted to assume that nature must have exhausted all its possible structural combinations and given form to every system of organization by which living material could be arranged. But we are constantly discovering new forms, new types of specialization that are unexpected and often extraordinary. Without the gleanings of fossil nature, we would have only a narrow view of the field of possibilities open to life in its endless adaptation to its environment.

Since the most elementary forms of life appeared over three billion years ago, life has worked its way by transformations and successive adaptations, taking many paths that have produced different beings destined for different fates. Some of these paths have been impasses, incapable of advancing evolution; other lines have known extraordinary development before becoming extinct for reasons still unknown; yet others persist to today in almost unchanged forms—these are "living fossils." And still other, more recent lines, are now in the process of expansion, such as birds, mammals, and man.

If living nature is endless in its renewals and evolution is irreversible, it nevertheless obeys various principles that are translated through the repetition of special models, solutions, and biological systems. These are, for example, the models of symmetry, segmentation, coiling, and articulation, the organisms' adaptive solutions to aquatic, terrestrial, and aerial life, and also the systems of symbiosis, parasitism, protection, and aggression. From these principles issue the many phenomena of homeomorphy (or convergence of form) which manifests itself throughout evolution as so many endpoints of specialization.

It is by studying these developments that we will one day perhaps be able to imagine the future's evolution.

87

Pentacrinus bollensis, *a Liassic echinoderm from Germany. Crinoids or "sea lilies" are animals that appeared during the Paleozoic era and formed vast underwater prairies. Several forms exist in today's oceans as true living fossils.*

Diversification of Structures and Forms

Living matter always presents itself according to a clear architecture and a well-ordered structure. This architectural order stems from the functional need for equilibrium, which is conditioned by perpetual exchanges of material and energy between living substances and their milieus.

Every organic structure can be studied on three different levels: the histological microstructure of tissues, the morphological structure of organs, and finally the organism's architectural plan.

Unicellular organisms or protista—some belonging to the plant kingdom, others to the animal—comprise a universe apart. They first appeared in the Precambrian period, and from the start presented an astonishing structural complexity. Some can secrete hulls (frustules or shells) made of limestone (in foraminifera), celluloid material (in certain dinoflagellates), or silica (in radiolaria and diatom). These shells offer complex architectures from which an unbelievable richness of forms is born. The test (shell) of foraminifera rolls up and encloses itself in regular and complicated structures. The extravagant decoration of radiolaria is a source of wonder to the micropaleontologist. And we must not forget the remarkable geometric plans of diatoms, and the striking hairs and horns bristling on the bodies of tiny dinoflagellate fossils.

The first multicellular organisms (which we know from the end of the Precambrian era, about 700 million years ago) are of extremely varied complexity. The juxtapositions of cells are grouped and differentiated according to the organs whose tissues they comprise. Each organ has its own histological microstructure, which can be found perfectly preserved after fossilization. The supporting organs (hard parts, shells, or skeletons) are far and away the most resistant to decay and of greatest interest to the paleontologist. Their microstructures are astonishingly varied, with the most complicated generally spawned by the simplest organisms. In numerous invertebrates, the material forming these hard parts distributes itself in granules, fibers, prisms, and sheets, which are often divided into layers. Light playing over microscopic sheets of aragonite in shells produces nacreous reflections, still visible in many fossilized specimens. There are unexpected types of microstructures, like the sponge's internal skeleton, a very complicated but regular network made of tiny spikelets of chalk or flint.

88

Architectural complexity rather than formal extravagance gives originality to the calcite shells of the different species of foraminifera. They can vary in size from 1/100 of a millimeter to more than 10 centimeters.

The small size of these elements and their complex, crowded interweaving—so astonishing to our eyes—gives the invertebrates' supporting organs cohesion and solidity. The skeletal tissue of vertebrates is simply masses of cells cloaked in a rigid substance. The true complexity is located, for them, on the level of the general structure.

In fact, each group of organized beings has its own structural "diagram," which forms a basis for the development of its many evolving and adaptive variations. The resulting forms often amaze us with their variety and originality. It is clear that the most primitive species always provide the simplest architectural plans, with complexity appearing only gradually. Thus the sea urchins of the Paleozoic era were regular and globular, while those dating from the Liassic period occur in unexpected forms (disc, heart-shaped, pyramidal), as their development entailed anatomical complications and thus morphological variations. The case of the gastropods is better known: if the living species stun us with their extraordinary shell forms, the first forms, emerging in the Cambrian period, were relatively simple and archaic. The helical winding of the shell was realized only later, permitting a luxury of forms that was itself the result of a growing complexity.

This morphological complexity is generally made possible by an underlying architectural complexity on the level of structures of articulation. Here also the possibilities are greater in the more advanced groups. Beginning with slabs arranged according to a 5-point symmetry, echinoderms give rise to forms as diverse as starfish, sea urchins, crinoids, and many others. This is not far from the case of the arthropods, in whom the same structural plan orders trilobites, insects, spiders, and crustaceans. The maximum structural variation is achieved in vertebrates (which appeared 140 million years after invertebrates) from an organizational plan at once simple and remarkably constant in its branchings—an axial skeleton with bilateral symmetry and cephalization. The vertebrates became diversified according to every possible environment of life, whether aquatic, terrestrial, or aerial. And for each mode of life we find a corresponding variation: there is a fish architecture, an amphibian architecture, one for reptiles, birds, and mammals. New structural possibilities appear in the interior of each order, to become increasingly specialized according to the level of evolution of the group. Mammals, the last to appear and still in full expansion, give a striking example of this in the transformations their members have undergone. All composed of

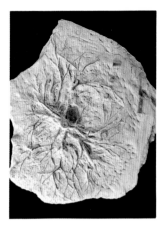

89

View of the top of a "root" of Eucalyptocrinus crassus, a Silurian period echinoderm from Indiana, in the United States. The adaptation of animal form to function can be wholly unexpected: while crinoids are animals, they have long "stalks," like plants, and they also have "roots" that solidly secure them to marine floors.

the same elements and articulations, they can fit themselves out according to forms as varied as the whale's fin, the horse's hoof, the bat's wing, and man's arm.

Symmetry and Segmentation

The etymology of symmetry means "with measure" or "just proportion." This notion is among the most important outcomes of the observation of nature, in which the regularity of certain forms gave birth to the idea of measurable relations among their different parts. Thus, man's imagination was struck by the regularity of flower petals, the structure of numerous fruits, the regular winding of shells, and naturally by the marvelous regularity of crystals.

But, like perfect geometric figures, rigorous symmetry is unknown in organic nature. So numerous are the examples of dissymmetry, that the rule of symmetry cannot be regarded as absolute. The bilateral symmetry of vertebrates is imperfect: the two sides of the human face, for example, are not absolutely identical; certain flat fish have eyes located on the same side of the median line. Examples of this sort abound in every living group.

But no matter how relative the application, the great principles of symmetry nevertheless direct the majority of beings, whether animals or plants. Theoretically, symmetry can be established in three ways: through relation to a point, an axis, or a plan.

Symmetry related to a point (realized when all the points of a body are correspondingly equidistant from a central point called the center of symmetry) does not actually occur in nature. Nevertheless many spores, grains, and fruits, as well as some very regular micro-organisms, approach it. In the hierarchy of animal organization, spheric form remains confined to poorly evolved beings.

Symmetry along an axis is obtained schematically by drawing a perpendicular from one point of the object to the axis, and by making it turn by a fraction so as to obtain a symmetrical point. The order of symmetry is the number of fractional turns required to return to the initial figure; thus the symmetry of a five-pointed star is said to be of the order five.

Axial symmetry is widespread in the plant world. Here we can note the symmetry of flowers, pollen grains, and fruits, generally of the orders three, five, and six. It is equally frequent among unicellular organisms, which secrete a chitinous, limestone, or silicous shell, such as diatoms with symmetry of the orders three, five, or infinite (in the disc form), or bilateral chalk coccoliths with orders of symmetry varying according to the species.

Coelenterates have symmetry of the orders six or eight. One can find very complicated figures among them by superimposing an axial symmetry secondary to an initial bilateral symmetry (as in the case of several sea anemones). Moreover, lower creatures present fewer elements of symmetry than more evolved beings.

Echinoderms furnish a classic example of order five symmetry: starfish points, the ambulacran zones of sea urchins, and the basal plaques of the calice of trinoids. Yet we should note that the order five, which occurs widely in living things, is unknown in crystalline systems, and the corresponding polyhedron is never encountered in minerology.

As for plane-based, or bilateral, symmetry, we can imagine it best through the image of an object reflected in a mirror. Though the simplest form to construct geometrically, it was originally the most widespread. We find it from the first stages of embryonic development, both in vertebrates and lower animal forms. Once the first stages are past, the embryo divides into a certain number of elements or metameres that display perfect bilateral symmetry, with each henceforth participating in the development of different organs. This bilateral symmetry remains central to branchings that develop along a longitudinal axis.

Metamerization often leaves visible traces in the adult form. Thus, among annelids (whose present-day forms are similar to those of the early Paleozoic era), metameres are represented in the rings of earthworms or the tapeworm's flattened segments. Similarly, among the arthropods, which were already well differentiated over 600 million years ago at the beginning of the Cambrian Period, segmentation linked to bilateral symmetry is especially visible, whether in distant trilobites, crustaceans, or insects. This original metamerization has also left traces in the organization of primitive mollusks like the monoplacophora, which have been known since the Cambrian period.

Complicated forms may develop. Sea urchin larvae have a bilateral symmetry on which the adult radial symmetry is superimposed after

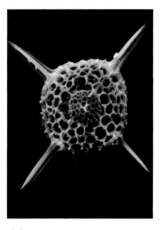

90

The siliceous shell of radiolarians becomes infinitely complicated after starting from a spherical form—there are thousands of varieties. The Hexacontium asteracanthion from the Quaternary period is structured as two latticed, enclosed spheres ornamented by four long spines.

complex metamorphoses. In vertebrates, which appeared more than 450 million years ago, the symmetrical plan is materialized in the dorsal supporting organ, the vertebral column, which contains the axis of the nerves. Segmentation in the embryo develops from one side of this central nervous tube to the other according to the same principle of bilateral symmetry. Symmetry according to a plane determines the tracery of most leaves in plants, as well as their veining, the arrangement of petals in certain flowers, and the structure of many fruits.

Thus symmetry, regulating every shape, appears as an undemonstrable but evident necessity. It builds living structures in an infinite variety of forms.

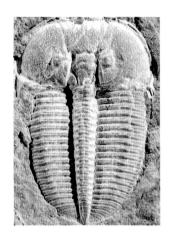

91

Trilobites, which are primitive marine arthropods from the Paleozoic era, have bodies composed of identical articulated segments built according to a clear bilateral symmetry. This is Aulacopleura konincki, *from the Silurian period in Bohemia.*

The Mathematical Laws Ordering Forms

"When God undertook the ordering of the universe . . . he began by distinguishing things according to form and number."

The scientific realism of the twentieth century is a far cry from Platonic metaphysics. But as clear as ever is the fact that contemplation often leads to feelings of beauty and harmony. This beauty stems from a formal perfection which is necessary because it is functional—*nothing* is gratuitous in nature.

The myriad forms to which nature lends itself are dominated by two geometrical figures, the spiral and the star. Numerous mollusks wind themselves according to spirals (on one level) or helices (three-dimensional versions of the spiral). The shell of foraminifera can also be a spiral. The horns of rams and wild sheep follow the same pattern. The "snail" of man's inner ear, or cochlea, describes a spiral wound up on a cone. The Epeire spider weaves a spiraling thread around star-shaped rays. Examples abound within the plant world: sunflower seeds arranged on the flower, the scales of pine cones and the pineapple, and daisy petals are shaped into opposing spirals. The arrangement of leaves on stems also follows a helical form.

The star shape (issuing from point-based symmetry) is another constant in nature, but one type is particularly striking: the 5-pointed star, which is the basis of many animal and plant forms. The tips of this star sketch a star-shaped regular pentagon. (One can also find the same pentagon by following the placement of leaves on a stem.) Here, complex mathematical relations intervene. The star-shaped pentagon is inscribed in a regular convex pentagon (obtained by joining the consecutive tips of the star). The relationship between the sides of the starred pentagon and the convex pentagon is a number called ϕ, equal to 1.618, which is found with a curious frequency in a whole series of mathematical ratios. Thus, a straight line can be divided into two parts such that the same ratio exists between the small section and the large as between the large and the whole. This ratio is always 1.618. One of its properties is as the cause of a unique geometric progression called the Fibonacci series, in which each term is equal to the sum of its two preceding numbers: 1, 2, 3, 5, 8, 13, and so on. The ratio of each number to the preceding one (13/8, 8/5 . . .) oscillates around 1.618. Now, in the winding of leaves around their stem, the angle formed by two consecutive leaves forms a fractional turn which is the ratio between two consecutive numbers in the Fibonacci series. This is the angle necessary for the maximum fall of sunshine on all leaves.

In the scales of the pine cone, either five spirals turn in one direction and eight in the other, or the same with eight and thirteen. In the flower of the Jerusalem artichoke, the numbers eighty-nine and one hundred forty-four are found; and so on with other plants. All these numbers form part of the Fibonacci series, and their ratio is 1.618.

There is still more. One can construct a sequence of squares, each having for its side length one of the Fibonacci series numbers. Beginning with a square with the side one, one adds another with the side one, then one with the side two, then three, five, eight, etc., turning regularly. The squares wind around according to a spiral called a logarhythmic or Bernouilli spiral. This is the spiral of mollusk shells, flower seeds, and almost all natural spirals. It forms the most harmonious growth curve in nature, because it always remains like to itself in its proportions throughout the course of its coiling. Thus the animal or plant can grow without changing forms, the reason for the spiral's existence in nature.

The number ϕ, 1.618, is called "the golden number." It was known to the ancient Greeks, who defined it mathematically, and was empirically perceived even at the beginning of distant antiquity. The monuments and works of art predating Hellenic civilization are rich in geometric figures linked to the golden number. Undoubtedly, the observation of natural structures was at the source of this intuitive notion.

The three points dividing a straight line in the described manner

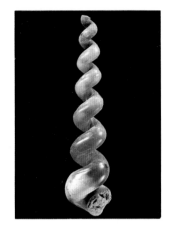

92

A fine example of a helix, the three-dimensional version of a logarithmic spiral formed by life is an internal cast of a Triassic period gasteropod from Germany, which comes to us fossilized in pure chalcedony.

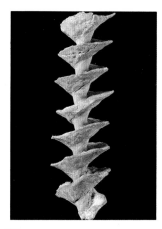

93

Several regularly wound forms that are not the result of logarithmic spirals can be formed in living nature. Here is Archimedipora archimedes, the result of an association between an algae and a sea moss. Its origin is the Mississippian period in Illinois, United States.

form the "Golden Section" or "divine proportion." The human body is partially constructed according to it—we find it in the proportions of the face, in the relationship between the height of the body (head to toe) and the distance from head to navel, between the joints of fingers and toes. This "divine proportion" permits, among other things, the marking of "golden rectangles" (in which the ratio between the two sides is 1.618), with the property of producing smaller golden rectangles when a square equal to the small side is removed. If, beginning with the initial golden rectangle, one takes away a succession of squares from each remaining rectangle, "Golden Sections" of increasingly small size are obtained. We can construct the famous logarhythmic spiral in their interiors.

From a strictly mathematical viewpoint, only an approximation of the golden number is found in nature. Nevertheless, it remains astonishingly close, and no other number is found with such constancy in the proportions of so many living beings. Kepler called it the "jewel of geometry."

Thus, a specific mathematical relation gives birth to an infinity of natural forms that never cease to astonish us. Here we reach the transition point between mathematics and living reality.

The Living Phenomenon and the Surprises of Biology

From primitive bacteria to man, passing through the innumerable stages of evolution, living matter has undergone more and more varied exigencies and increasingly complicated functions that are themselves consequences of its extraordinary development on earth. With specialization of cells, which first permitted differentiated tissues and then organs, life has gradually enlarged its aptitudes until it has expanded over the entire surface of the globe. In many animals that today are extinct, the examples of adaptive specialization and the corresponding morphological types seem more unexpected than extreme. The large reptiles of the Mesozoic era offer some of the most spectacular and best known examples.

Adaptation may seem one of the most important factors in biological diversification, but it is not the only one: adaptation is no more than a species' ability to respond favorably to the constraints of its surrounding milieu. Natural selection, which aims at eliminating those individuals least capable of self-maintenance, also plays a large role in the specialization of organisms. Mutation, which brings about the appearance of new and persistent genetic traits in a species, could be equally responsible for numerous morphological innovations. In fact, these three factors probably act jointly, mutation developing only if propitious to adaptation and favored by natural selection.

Convergences of form, which are particularly clear in marine vertebrates, correspond to adaptations. Adaptation to an aquatic milieu has produced a hydrodynamic body, not only in fish, but also in secondary reptiles with fins like the ichthyosaurus, in marine mammals like the dolphin and whale, and in diving birds, even though these animals descend from very distinct lines of evolution. Examples of this type are as abundant in fossil nature as in modern life, in plants as in invertebrates and vertebrates.

The vertebrates have occupied many environments, and adaptations to swimming, flight, the chase, jumping, and so on, are the result. For highly specialized regional diets, we find corresponding differentiations, not only in teeth or in the beaks of birds, but in cranial, skeletal, and muscular anatomy. Other differentiations are related to climate, to the dominant color of the environment, or to the types of neighboring species.

In this fascinating field of biological evolution, each discovery must be regarded as an event that helps us to determine the varied paths of evolutionary change. If our curiosity has been awakened by the progression of these evolutionary lines, how much more moving are the testimonies of human antecedents: Australopithecans, Pithecanthropans, Neanderthals. More than intermediary forms, they represent specialized lateral branches of the hominoid line. Each presents a stage in progressive humanization, marked by a gradual augmentation of intelligence in increasingly determined forms. Thanks to patient paleontological research, we can not only gather "flashes of intuition" on the creatures of the past, but can also acquire a dynamic vision of the evolving continuum.

94

A remarkable link in the chain of evolution is the Archaeopteryx, *from the Upper Jurassic of Bavaria, Germany. The intermediary between reptiles and birds,* Archaeopteryx *had typically reptilian characteristics, such as jaws with teeth, a long vertebral tail, and paws with four members, coexisting with traits unique to birds, such as wings and plumage.*

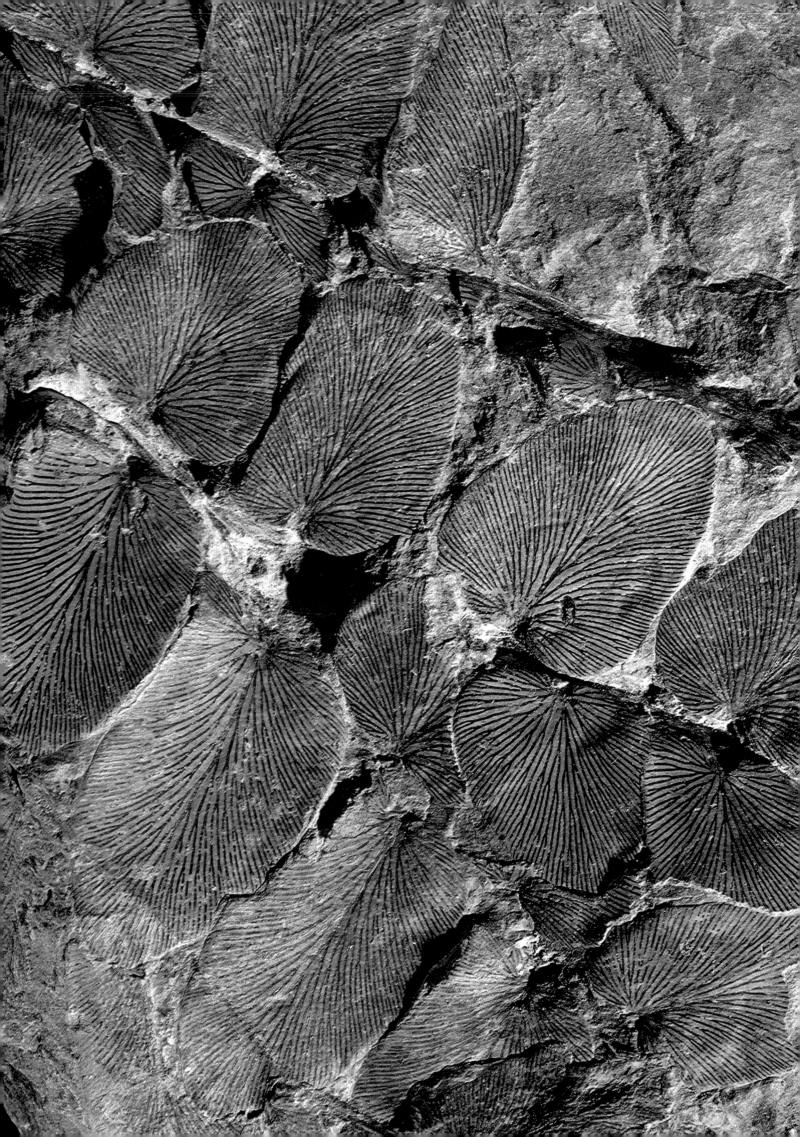

Extinct Forms and Living Fossils

Among the millions of forms produced by evolution over millions of years, some have definitely disappeared, others have gradually been modified, and others—far rarer—have remained almost identical to their original forms.

Each geological period has seen the predominance of particular groups distinct from their predecessors and successors. The immense Paleozoic forests saw the expansion of bracken, arborescent ferns, with trunks often forty meters high, along with equisetales, today, horsetails, and pteridospermaphyta, astonishing "seed ferns" of majestic bearing.

Strange armored fish, often with fearful-looking jaws, were developing in the oceans. In the depths, the trilobites grew plentiful; their neighbors were gigantostraca, fierce aquatic arthropods armed with sturdy pincers of which the largest, *Pterugotus*, was two meters long. None of these forms was to see the dawn of the Mesozoic era after an existence of tens of millions of years.

The Mesozoic era witnessed the explosive development and total extinction of the ammonites, which disappeared for unknown reasons leaving the remains of over 10,000 species. Their famous contemporaries, the dinosaurs, occupied every ecological niche with highly specialized and often strangely adapted forms and a gigantism as legendary as their ferocity. Often more than twenty meters long, they spread throughout the earth, then disappeared entirely at the end of the Cretaceous period. Other large flesh-eating marine reptiles disappeared during the same period. These were the long-jawed ichthyosaurs and the plesiosaurs, hoisting necks with seventy-six vertebrae. Not one of these ferocious and spectacular forms survived to the end of the Mesozoic era. Many other strange creatures haunted this period, and all were extinguished.

The Tertiary era saw the gradual re-establishment of living flora and fauna. Most of the groups that appeared at this time still have living descendents today. The most astonishing of those that disappeared are perhaps the giant, disquieting birds that were finally killed by man: *Diatyrma* in the Eocene, *Phororhacus* in the Miocene, and in the Quaternary the *Aepyornis* from Madagascar and *Dinornis* from New Zealand.

South America, which had long been isolated, sheltered a crowd of very special mammals that finally succumbed to the invasions of North

95

A frond from Neuropteris speciosa, a pteridosphermaphyte from the Carboniferous period in France. For lack of a better term, these strange plants were christened "grainy ferns." They were common to the Carboniferous forests which, after expanding throughout the earth, finally became extinct at the beginning of the Cretaceous period.

American carnivores at the end of the Tertiary period. Whole families of marsupials, quite as numerous and diversified as their replacement placentalia, disappeared once and for all. In the Quaternary it was a time for strange, toothless creatures like the shell-bearing glyptodon.

The largest terrestrial mammal, *Baluchitherium*, a type of Asiatic rhinoceros six meters tall, became extinct during the Miocene epoch. As for the caveman's contemporary, the mammoth, it is the least known of a series of fossil elephants that followed one after the other from the Eocene epoch up to present times.

If it is exalting to imagine these vanished forms, how much more moving it is to discover real "living fossils" arising intact from the depths of geological ages. Relic forms of invertebrates abound. The graceful nautilus comes to us straight from the end of the Cambrian period. Crinoids, or water lilies, were already undulating at the water's will in the Silurian seas. Among arthropods, the king crab, covered by a shell shield and bearing a long sting, has not varied since the Triassic period. Scorpions and spiders were already swarming 350 million years ago, and dragonflies from the lithographic limestones of Solnhofen (Jurassic period) are found to this day in Japan.

Fish immediately recall the coelacanthe (*Latimeria chalumnae*). Known to have existed since the Devonian period, coelacanthes were thought to have disappeared 70 million years ago in the Cretaceous period, until one was caught in 1938. Many have been found since then in the archipelago of the Comoro Islands. There are still several rare living specimens of strange fish with lungs from the Devonian waters.

Amphibians also have a living fossil, a strange giant salamander inhabiting Asia and unchanged since the Miocene epoch. Another amphibian relic lives in the caverns of Yugoslavia; this is the olm (proteus), which is remarkably similar to its Eocene ancestor and, like it, retains gills. We can find replica of the "monsters" of the Mesozoic era in these living reptiles: our three types of crocodiles became individualized after the Cretaceous period; the strange New Zealand sphenodon, the unique example of a group that flourished during the Mesozoic, has not altered one bit since the Jurassic; giant turtles from the Galapagos and Seychelle Islands remind us astonishingly of those of the Tertiary period.

Mammals have a number of surprises in store for us. The African forest is the home of the strange okapi, the survivor of Miocene and Pliocene types. In the same environment lives the remarkable oryx,

96

Having emerged in the Carboniferous period, spiders traversed the geological eras without obstruction before adapting to the environment shared with man. Found in Baltic amber, this one—despite its 30 million years—is extremely close to today's spiders.

which became specialized after the Miocene. A small lemurian, the aye-aye, has taken refuge in Madagascar as the survivor of a family extinct for 25 million years. As for the tarsier, a primate from the Indonesian forests, its nearest relatives lived 50 million years ago.

We must not forget the desman, an insect-eating mammal related to the mole ,and living in the Pyrenean streams, which is now becoming extinct after enduring continuously for 20 million years following the Miocene epoch.

Marsupials are entirely a relic order. These mammals, which are extremely ancient and have been differentiated since the Cretaceous period, underwent an extraordinary expansion before taking refuge in Australia and South America. Many other forms are today no more than survivors, whether their representatives are poorly evolved and preserve most of their primitive characteristics, or whether they have maintained their archaic qualities, making them hard to classify along current lines of evolution. Anteaters and duckbill platypuses are oviparous mammals. The kiwi is a wingless, tailless bird, and the hoazin has wings equipped with claws.

How have so many creatures avoided the course of evolution? Most of them have lived in particularly propitious environments—in tropical forests, caverns, oceans, and very isolated islands. But the speed of evolution related to each line of descent also has its own effect. It can be so slow that it seems entirely arrested, as with the coelacanthe; or specialization can be so precocious, so fast, that it quickly ends with its full realization—such is the case of the tarsier. Many explanations have been attempted, and causes well researched. But numerous unknowns still exist.

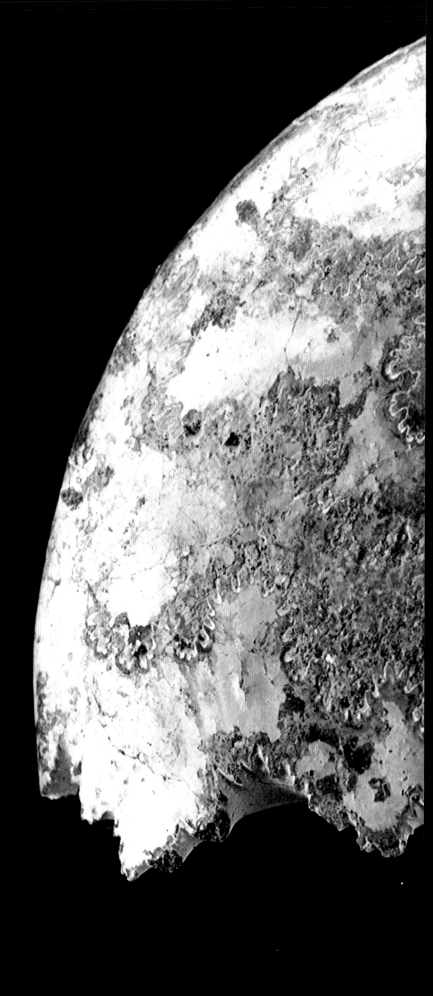

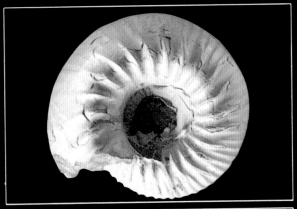

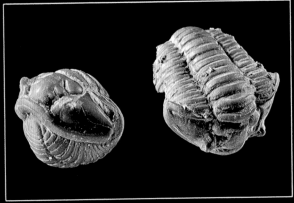

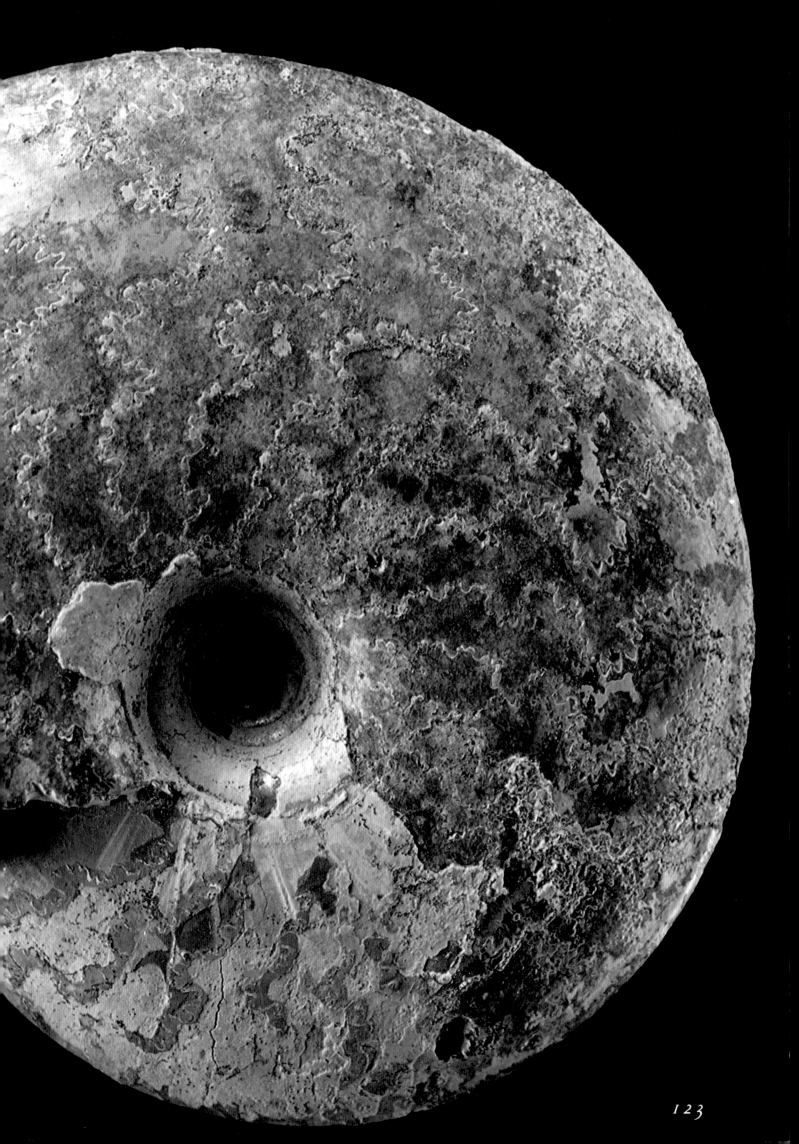

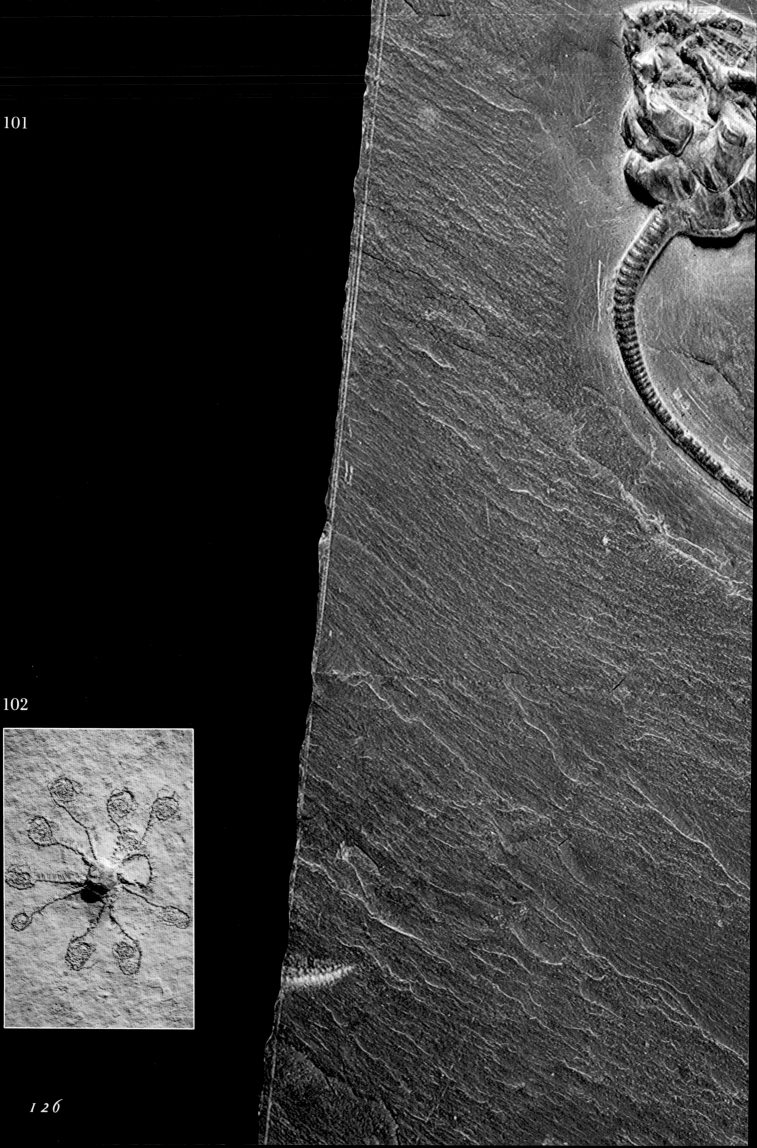

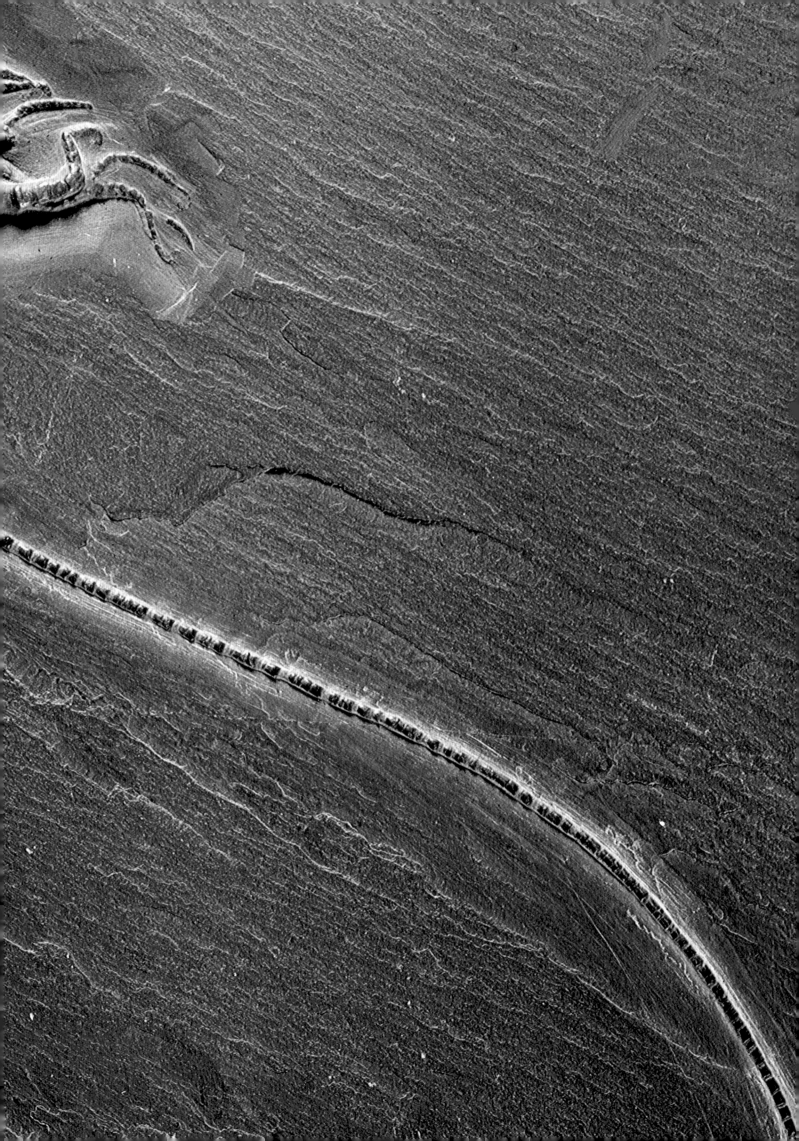

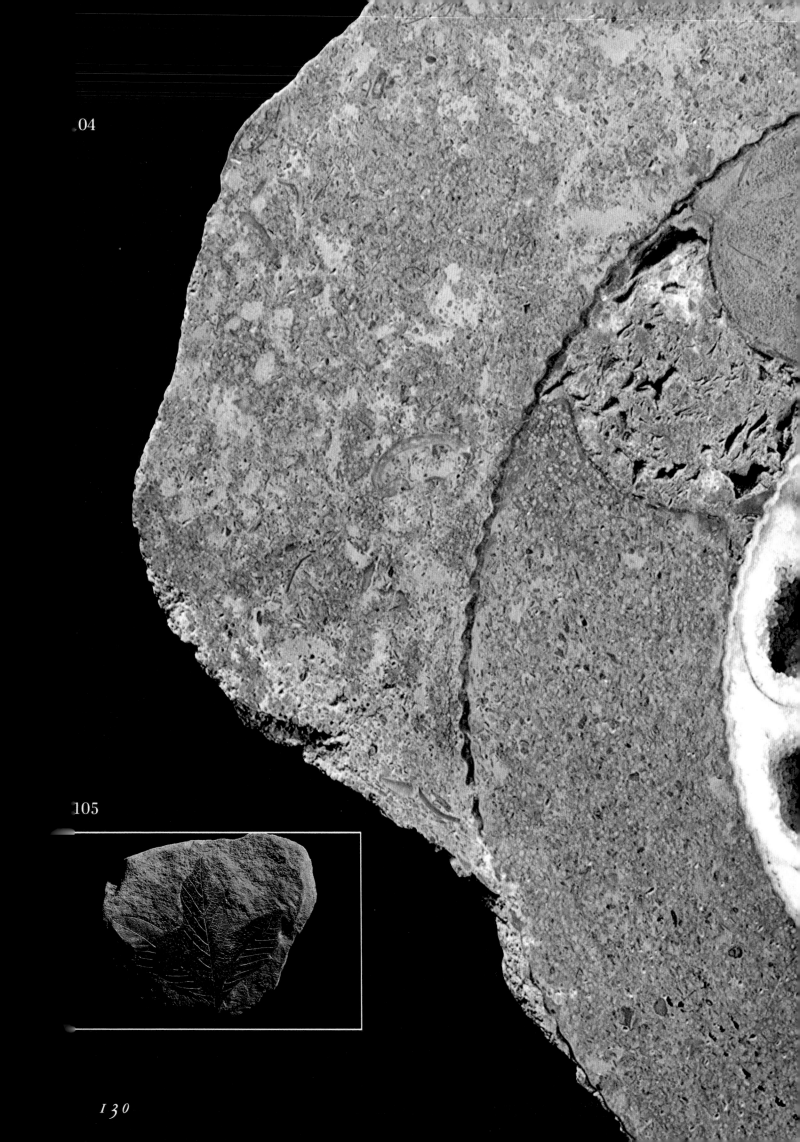

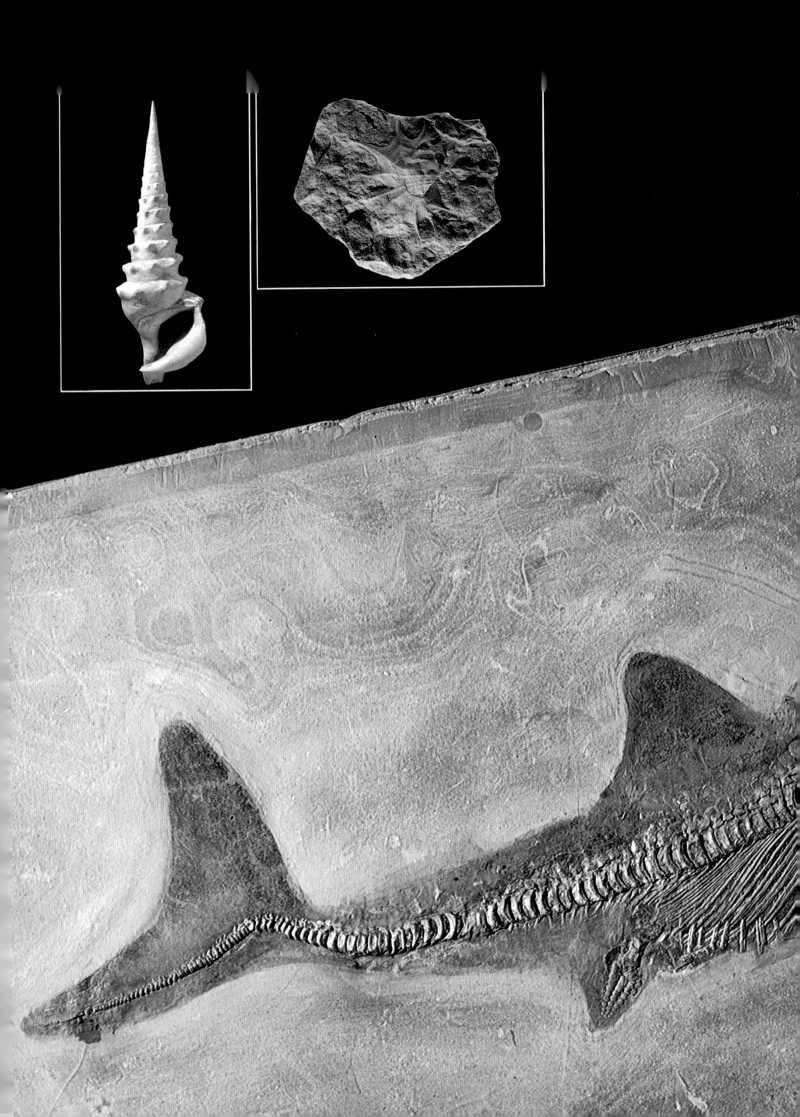

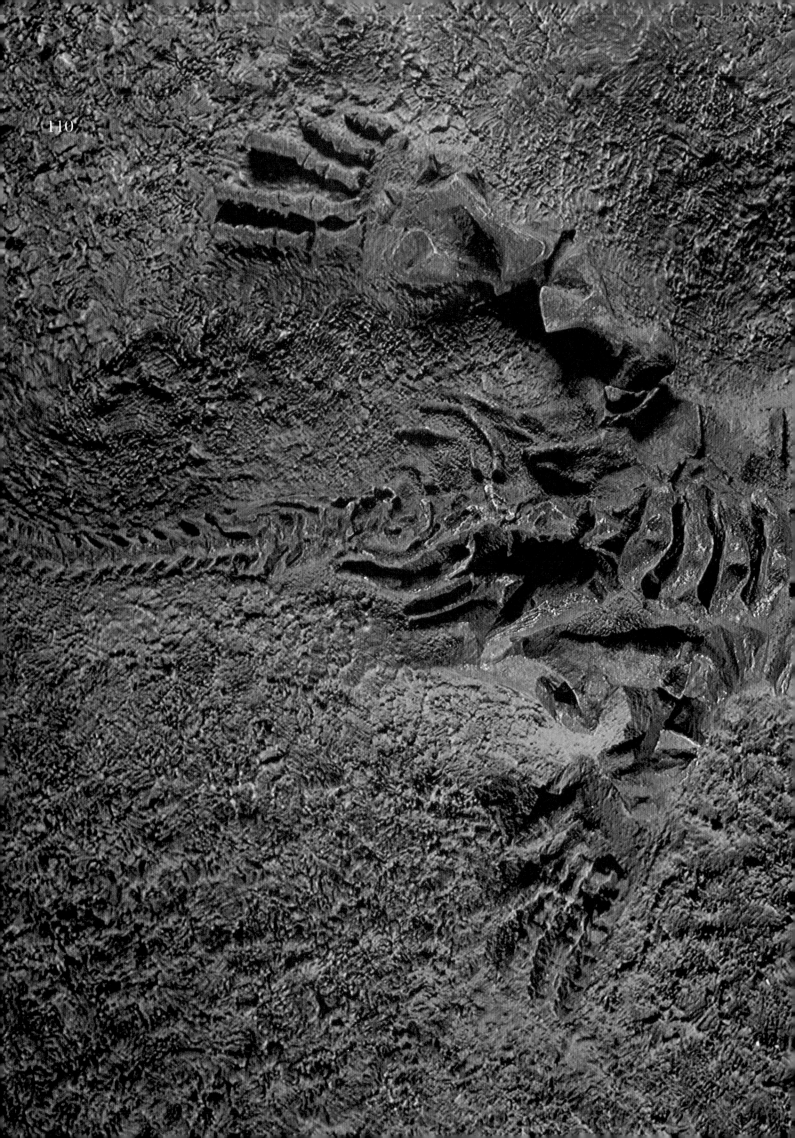

112

113

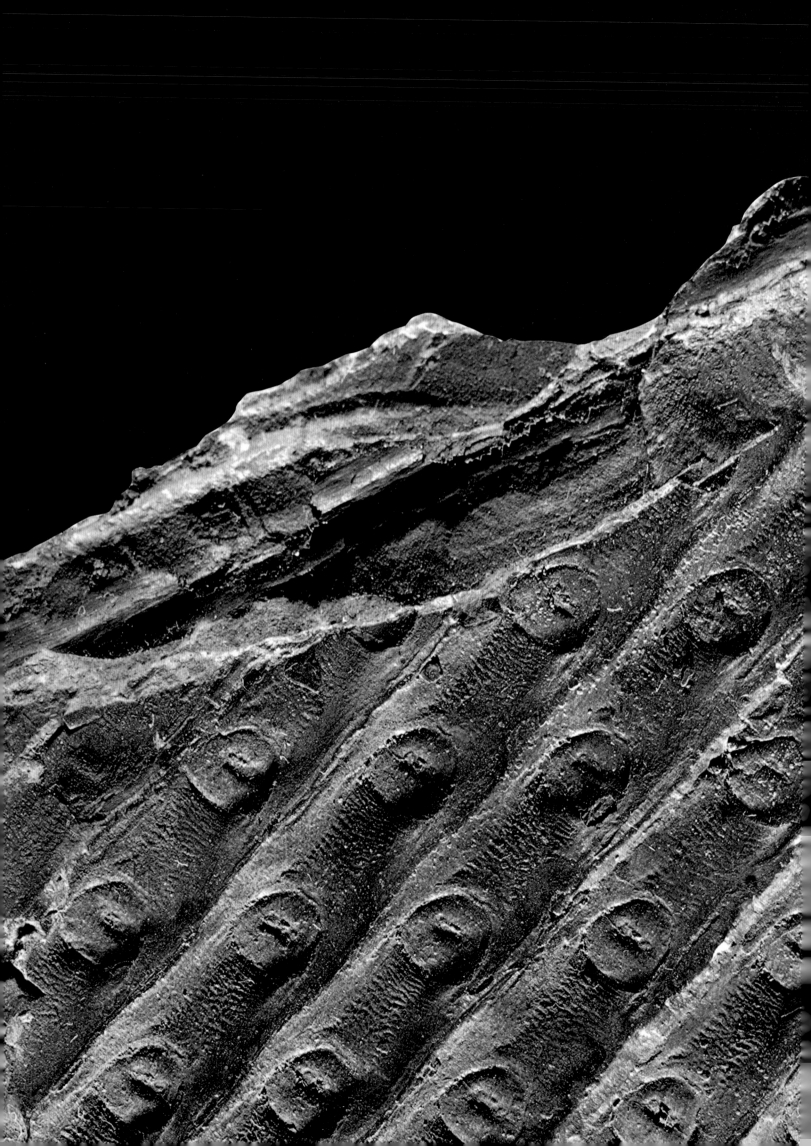

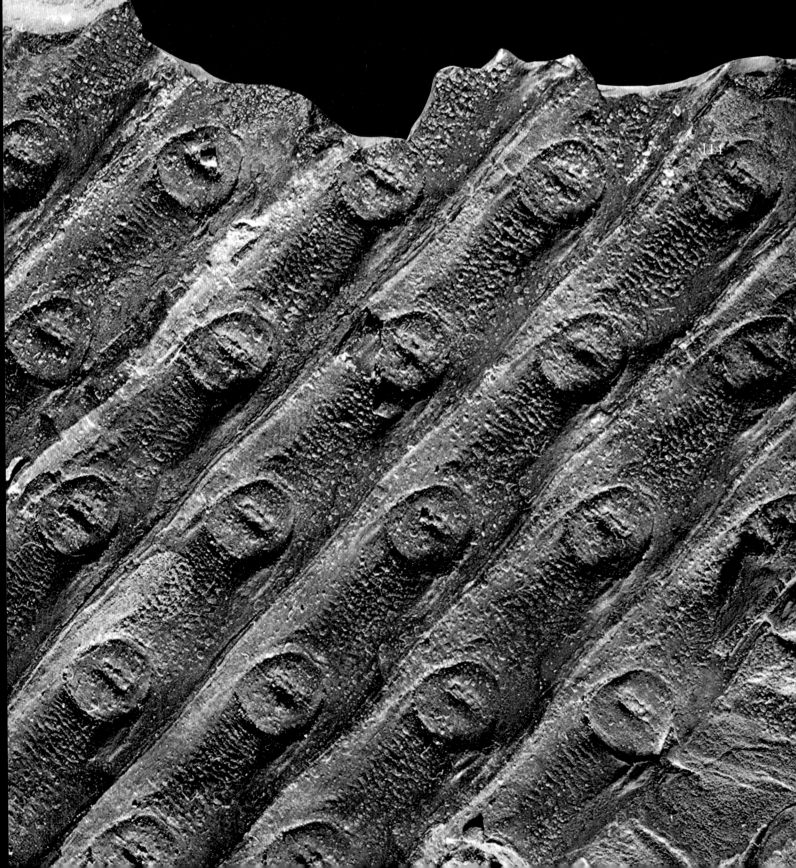

4. *The Measure and Immeasurability of Terrestrial Time*

From when shall we date the earth's constitution? What are the dates of the first stages of life? How long has man himself existed? These are only so many questions whose importance we can measure by the anguish often aroused by predictions of an eventual "end of the world."

Though fossil study cannot help us to predict the future, it can shed precious light on the way the terrestrial environment evolves, on the different stages that have dominated life's history, and on the varied phenomena of the past and present, whose effects can be partially inferred. Above all, fossils give us an image of the immensity of geological time, which in turn impels our most grandiose conception—modern man, identical to us in form, has existed for 37,000 years, and 3,300,000 years have passed since the beginnings of primitive humanity! This is an enormous amount of time, but small in view of the 185 million years since the first mammals appeared. It seems still less if we think of the 3 billion years required for the development of our present era, starting from the first germs of life realized on our planet.

In the scale of geological time, there is no common measure between the duration of human enterprise or civilizations and the duration of a species, line of descent, or general class of organisms. But all this, we might say, is too far removed from us and too disproportionate to touch our imaginations. Time is immaterial, inordinate, and intangible.

To this, geologists as well as paleontologists reply that time can be seen and touched as concretely as the stones of a building. It is enough to consider the Triassic beds located on Cape St. Andre in Madagascar, with deposits of alternating red and yellow strata. The former, filled with hematite, correspond to dry seasons, while the latter, yellowed by limonite, correspond to humid weather. Two consecutive strata thus indicate a year of sedimentation, and 50,000 double strata have been deposited in this way. What could be more concrete than the 50,000 years so displayed, open to our eyes like archival files extending through 200 million years!

Terrestrial time is registered in this way, with often remarkable accuracy, by the fossils and sediments that record it. Tens of kilometers of geological layers, species following species in numerous lines of descent: here is the most tangible way to show the matchless duration of the phenomena from which we have issued.

And yet we have only a partial record of the geological and paleontological scale. Sedimentation has not been continuous everywhere and

115

Acrioceras tabarelli, *an ammonite from the Lower Cretaceous period in France. The ammonite group lasted 330 million years, from the middle of the Paleozoic era to the end of the Mesozoic when it disappeared abruptly, having given rise to several thousand species through time.*

many species—the missing links of evolution—have escaped fossilization. Such "lacunae" in sedimentation and fossilization have been as frequent in marine as in continental areas, and allow us to estimate that the absences are quantitatively higher than the preserved remains.

The Recoil of Known Time

As recently as three centuries ago, people were accustomed to admitting, in accordance with Genesis, that all Creation (earth, firmament, oceans, plants, animals, and man) had been accomplished in six days.

In 1650, the Irish archbishop James Ussher concluded, after studying the Bible, that the Creation had occurred on October 26, 4004 B.C., a date that was for a long time taken on faith, and still is by many fundamentalist believers.

In 1729, when fossils were routinely interpreted as results of the Biblical Flood, the naturalist Louis Bourget was not afraid to advance the notion that "sixteen centuries" had flowed "between Creation and the Flood." Before him, in 1695, John Woodward had dated the Flood at 250 years prior to the Egyptian pyramids.

The Bible's influence imposed on earth history a strict chronology. Since it extended back only some 6,000 years, it considerably restricted the dates of appearance of living creatures. Nevertheless, at the end of the seventeenth century some minds were already thinking that the earth's history must have been far longer.

One idea of the vast duration of geological time (though a very approximate one) was to see the light of day with Buffon who, in the *Epochs of Nature* (1778), gave the earth an age of at least 75,000 years: "One would sense that this enormous duration of 75,000 years is still not large enough for all of nature's great works, whose construction shows us that they could only have been made by a slow succession of ordered and constant movements." Imagining the time required to deposit sedimentary beds and transform fossils, Buffon felt the need to pull back "the limit of this time, too immense for the imagination and nevertheless too short for our judgement." This was the beginning of the ladder of geological time.

In 1830, Charles Lyell stimulated awareness of the earth's great age and its different stages by calculating its duration not only in thousands, but in millions of years. In the same stroke he defined the principle of geological chronology: since the same types of fossils existed in contemporary sediments, the earth's strata could be dated according to these characteristic fossils. Lyell estimated the beginning of the Primary period to be 240 million years ago, which was a decisive step in the reconstruction of known time.

But the possibility of appreciating our planet's age was considerably limited by the fragmentary and uncertain evidence of the earth's oldest sedimentations. Many methods of dating were tested, some based on the earth's cooling time and providing no satisfactory conclusions, others based on the time needed for oceans to acquire their current salt levels and giving primitive oceans an age of 300 million years. Geologists in turn came to measure the total thickness of these gradually accumulated sedimentary deposits. It was found to be about 50 kilometers! Calculations taking account of the characteristic speed of accumulation for limestones, sands, and clay were made which resulted in figures of approximately 500 to 600 million years for the entire duration of geological time. Thus we were constantly led to push backwards the primordial events of our planet, while new paleontological discoveries forced the extension of life's supposed origins always further into time.

It was necessary to await the discovery of radioactivity and the development of physico-chemical methods of dating, for a new stage to be reached. Most bodies are composed of radioactive elements (isotopes) which are broken down and transformed with time. Each radioactive isotope has its own disintegration period corresponding to the time needed to transform half its material. Thus carbon-14 is transformed according to a period of 5,730 years; uranium-234 has a half-life of 250,000 years; that of helium-4 is 4.5 billion years. By measuring the amount of a radioactive isotope remaining in a body, taking account of its disintegration period, one can calculate the object's age.

The techniques based on isotopic analysis were difficult to establish and today still present many hazards. After numerous approximations, these techniques now allow us to assign an age of 600 million years to the beginning of the Paleozoic era and approximately 4.5 billion years to the consolidation of the earth's crust. Simultaneously, discoveries of the first examples of life multiplied, with the first identified dating from around 3.1 billion years.

Twentieth-century man accepts the incalculable age of the earth and life as easily as the vastness of interplanetary distances. But one must imagine the problems Lyell's contemporaries had only a century ago in displacing notions drawn directly from the Bible and arriving at such important conceptions.

Fossils, "Markers" of the Past

Though the material components of rocks are generally not characteristic of a particular era (sands, limestones, and clay have been deposited at numerous times), fossils, in contrast, provide true markers of geological time. The findings of paleontology, in fact, provide our major references for reconstructing the chronology of terrestrial sediments.

The evolution of life forms, as manifested in the interconnecting morphology of organisms, provides a decisive criteria for establishing divisions in the layers of the terrain, as well as in the identification of stratigraphic "landmarks." The evolution of organisms allows for differences to appear which justify movement into new eras, new periods, new stages, or substages.

The most important divisions correspond to the appearance or disappearance of whole groups, indicating major modifications in environmental conditions. Thus, passage from the Mesozoic to Tertiary periods is marked by the extinction of ammonites and dinosaurs as the nummulites abruptly took over the seas; the first irregular echinoids appeared with the Jurassic period; the flowering plants (angiosperms) flourished at the beginning of the Cretaceous period.

Within each period, the distinctions between stages rest on less important facts, such as the appearance of new genera. The substages or "zones" are marked only by the succession of new species, or by changes in the nature or specific associations (the predominance of species or characteristic populations).

Thus, within the four geological eras we can count more than 300 substages or distinct zones, divided into some 80 stages of varying length. The gradual diversification of organisms and the growing complexity of their structures have resulted in increasingly fine divisions in sedimen-

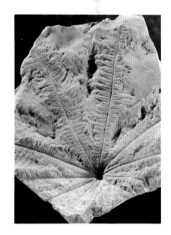

116

Among ferns, which have existed as a group since the Devonian period, several genera are characteristic of particular geological periods, like this Filicale, Dictyophyllum nathorsti. *It was gathered in Tonkin and is typical of the base of the Jurassic period.*

tary layers as we approach the present time. Thus, the Paleozoic era lasted 370 million years, while the Mesozoic extends only 165 million years; the Tertiary era represents less than 65 million years; and the Quaternary, according to certain estimates, began only 2.5 million years ago.

Through our deepened knowledge of fossils, we can not only date the layers of the terrains, but also can establish stratigraphic correlations over a distance, since the discovery of the same species in different places permits identification of the age. These correlations extend, with varying precision, from one continent to another and throughout the duration of geological time. Although their value is still uncertain for the most distant periods, they become increasingly precise as the stratigraphic layer becomes finer in its subdivisions.

From this point of view, all fossil groups are not equally interesting. Good indicators, called "characteristic fossils," are those whose geographic extension, frequency, and short periods of development mark off the same level of development with sure strokes. "Poor fossils" (a term sanctioned by use), which exist throughout time without notable modification, are also found; such is the case of the cockroach, practically unchanged since its appearance in the Paleozoic era.

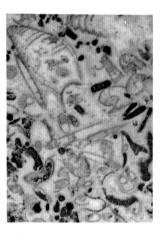

117

This polished limestone of Belgian origin can be accurately dated thanks to the fossils it contains, namely, Orthoceratites calamiteus, a nautiloid characteristic of the Devonian period.

Permanence and Discontinuities of Life

The doctrine of "global revolutions," which Cuvier promoted in the early nineteenth century, attributed the interruptions in earthly life to a series of catastrophes and successive re-creations. Today we know, thanks to the illuminations of evolutionary theories, that life has moved constantly onward since environmental conditions became adequate for nurturing the first plant and animal populations. But the expansion of life has not, for all that, flowed with constancy throughout the duration of geological time. Its gradual development has been marked by fits and starts affecting epochs, areas, or entire classes of organisms. From such irregularities flow important variations in the speed of propagation, evolution, or diversification of organisms.

Certain transitional epochs like those at the boundaries of the Paleozoic and Mesozoic eras have been marked by declines in continental and marine flora and fauna which were probably due to important changes in the environment. Other periods, in contrast, have known rapid growth of plant and animal populations, as in the Middle and Upper Jurassic periods, when many new forms were diversified.

Though to a lesser degree than the boundaries of eras or periods, the limits of geological stages also correspond to perturbations in evolutionary dynamics and the progression of life, which are generally linked to sharp modifications in the milieu. Alongside these more or less generalized planetary accidents, all the regions of the world have known conditions in which life could not maintain itself, or in which it found itself reduced to several forms that were tolerant of or appropriate to extreme specialization. Such is the case today of the Sahara, which has endured as a desert for several millenia while regions in comparable latitudes were the chosen homes of extraordinary plant and animal life. Similarly, we find rich deposits of fossil organisms in the geological series of the same region, alternating with others that are totally or almost totally barren. But these are only local interruptions, life having developed in other regions. To these temporary modifications are added the many sedimentary interruptions that have intervened at more or less related intervals in all the geological series of the earth. They present so many lacunae, so many missing "pages" from the annals of fossil nature.

Another order of phenomena can be imputed to temporal rhythms in evolution, and results in striking distortions in the arrangement of the varied fossil types. As a general rule, evolution unfolds in a gradual manner. Beginning with a few slowly transforming species, the lines of evolution develop quite suddenly and are more and more rapidly enriched by new types which take over new territories (what is called "adaptive radiation") to later become stabilized and decline. Several offshoots can endure to become the departure points for new lines. The reptiles, appearing in the Carboniferous period, became spectacularly diversified in the Jurassic and Cretaceous periods, to leave behind them only a few impoverished lines. Similarly mammals, which timidly appeared at the end of the Triassic, were to remain "primitive" for approximately 280 million years before achieving their astonishing adaptive radiation in the Tertiary period.

Thus we can note sudden proliferations of new forms with largely unknown ancestral types appearing in geological series. We can also see the rather abrupt disappearance of entire groups that had formerly flourished. These "renewals" of flora and fauna, both marine and terrestrial, are not related to interruptions in the biological continuum but correspond to "growth crises" in evolution, often preceded or followed by phases less favorable to the expansion of life.

The Relativity of Terrestrial Time

Terrestrial time, which we calculate in years of 365 days, in days of 24 hours, and in hours of 60 minutes, and which appears to us as an inalterable dimension, rigorously regulated by the sidereal clock, seems relative when compared to planetary phenomena. Actually, the length of the day has varied constantly since the time our planet was first placed in orbit.

Astronomers state that the speed of the earth's rotation never stops decreasing, at a deceleration of two seconds each 100,000 years. And modern atomic clocks confirm with extreme accuracy that days are lengthened about 2/1,000 of a second every century. This variation seems slight on the scale of human societies, but on the scale of planetary time it is extremely important. According to this measure, primitive earth would have completed a full turn in less than half the time it takes today, and at the beginning of the Cambrian period, over 600 million years ago, a day's length would have equaled 21 hours.

Without judging the variations in the speed of the earth's revolution around the sun, as a function of progressive distance, the number of days in a solar year is also always decreasing. There would have been 425 days per year at the beginning of the Cambrian period, and about 380 at the beginning of the Mesozoic era.

The paleontologist is concerned with this gradual lengthening of the terrestrial day since the periodicity of the radiation received by our planet influences all biological rhythms, as well as the cell levels in tissues, organs, organisms, and groups of individuals. Photoperiodicity is responsible for the varied "internal rhythms" that direct the regulation of organisms by acting on the rhythms of growth and reproduction. These "internal rhythms" are unique to living matter, and are both acquired and transmitted by heredity. Theoretically they function in a pure state, independent of all exterior influences, but in fact they are modified and largely synchronized according to cosmic rhythms, adjusting themselves in daily, monthly, seasonal, and annual periods.

Hence, we appreciate the time we "live" through reference to our physiological and psychological rhythms, which are themselves adapted to daily and hourly rhythms. The superimposition of these two necessities, the one of very immediate incidence, the other more distant in effect and slow in fluctuation, lets us catch a glimpse of the relativity of terrestrial time.

The Times of Life

Physical Evolution

One geophysics theory teaches us that at the time of its formation—some 4.5 billion years ago—the earth must have had a diameter almost half its present diameter and a density of approximately 35 (as opposed to 5.5 today). The initial surface of the globe must thus have approached 200 million square kilometers, a number almost equal to the total surface of today's continents with the addition of plateaus and continental slopes.

The primitive crust was relatively thin and had a temperature still close to that required for fusion. It was mainly composed of silicon, aluminum, and magnesium (today the essential elements of its deep crust) and was shaped into a single continent with simply sketched fragments and barely accentuated reliefs. At the time, there were neither oceans nor atmosphere, but rather a "pneumatosphere," a sort of mist composed of hydrogen, ammonia, and water vapor, and formed largely by the degasification of the planet. This primitive pneumatosphere was totally without oxygen in a free state, and presented a screen against most solar rays. Hence it was ill-equipped to insure the birth and development of life.

The first seas formed by the gradual condensation of water vapor were vast, thin layers of muddy liquid sprawling over rock deserts largely unaccentuated by mountains, but pierced by volcanic fissures. The first

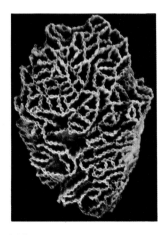

118

Halysites catenularia, *a tabulate coral found in Kentucky, lived 410 million years ago in the reefy depths of Silurian seas, where it was subject to a daily rhythm more rapid than today's. Years, at that time, had 400 days.*

oceanic depressions were formed very slowly as receptacles of surface waters and areas of accumulation for the very first geological sediments, then rich in iron. The same period witnessed the dissociation of the principal continental sheets and the first mountain ranges.

We estimate that the separation of the primitive pneumatosphere occurred around 3.8 billion years B.P. (before the present), breaking into a hydrosphere, represented by the oceanic mass, and an atmosphere without free oxygen, but permeable by solar rays, especially ultraviolet ones. The prevailing conditions led to the synthesis of numerous chemical compounds through the action of ultraviolet rays and the violent electrical discharges then troubling the earth's surface. Substances like amino acids and pyrimidines (the building blocks of organic matter, obtainable outside of life and in the absence of free oxygen) could have been constituted in the warm, muddy waters of Precambrian times. Recent experiences and observations of volcanic lavas, meteorites, and deep oceanic gullies show that the formation of organic molecules in these conditions is not purely by chance; on the contrary, the molecules issue from inescapable thermodynamic processes linked to a primordial phase in the chemical development of the compounds comprising organic matter.

Biological Evolution

This initial phase gave way, around 3.1 billion years B.P., to a further phase, called biological evolution, which corresponds to the emergence of what is properly called life.

At the atomic level, there is no difference between animate and inanimate matter, since they are both composed of the same elementary particles. It is only on the level of large molecules that a difference appears. Thus we can locate the beginning of life in the appearance of molecules sufficiently complex to respond to the needs of self-preservation, self-regulation, and self-maintenance, since the phenomenon of life is determined by the abilities of living creatures in the functions of assimilation, growth, and reproduction.

The phase of biological evolution of organic compounds was marked by the emergence of a cellular membrane. We do not know how

119

This 410- million year-old limestone fragment comes to us from the Silurian terrain around Dudley in England. It illustrates the appearance of an ocean bottom fossilized with many of its organisms: branching bryozams in conjunction with corals, brachiopods, crinoids, and trilobites.

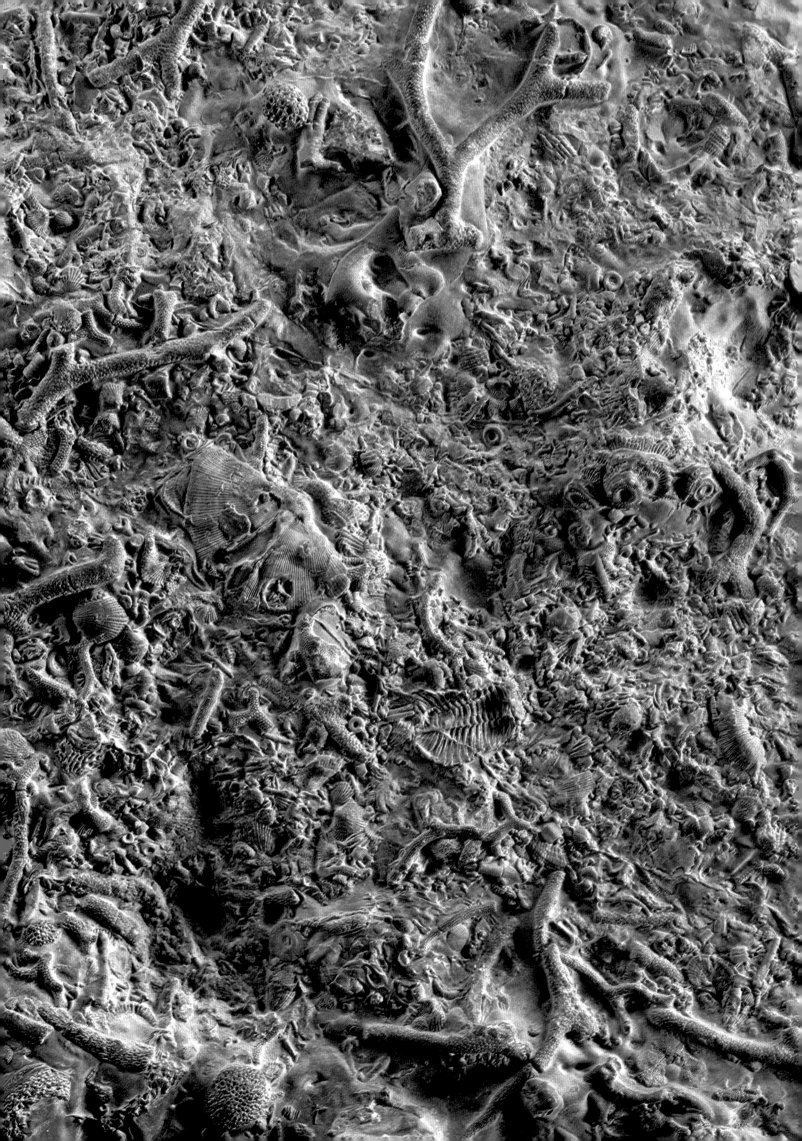

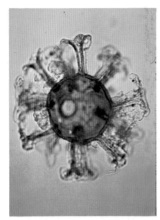

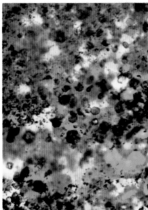

120, 121

Palaeocryptidium, *the small spheres of organic matter from the Precambrian sandstones of Brittany, and Baltisphaeridium, from the Silurian period of Eastern Prussia. Such acritarchs, often covered with horny material and not mineralized, are among the most primitive unicellular beings we know.*

122

Pecopterus crenata, *an arborescent fern growing in the immense Carboniferous swamps around Sarrebrück, Germany. The producer of oxygen and nutritive matter, the plant world preceded and has always accompanied the development of animal life.*

many lapses in time, how many failed efforts or repetitions were needed to achieve the first rough outlines of living cells. The oldest that have come down to us belong to the family of eobacteria, actually protocaryote cells, (without differentiated nuclei). We find them in formations dating from 3.1 billion years ago, which coincide with the first ores of striped iron.

Chlorophyll, the primordial substance of living phenomena, was one of the first molecules to be synthesized in the heart of watery regions rich·in carbon, nitrogen, and magnesium. And we know that chlorophyll has the property of transforming light into chemical energy able to direct the synthesis of glucose, beginning from carbonic acid and water with the emission of free oxygen (photosynthesis). The appearance of chlorophyll and photosynthesis can be dated at around 2.7 billion years B.P. The consequences of this event were little by little to transform planetary conditions; chlorophyll was to permit the growth and development of plants, and free oxygen was gradually to enrich the atmosphere.

The first known plants were unicellular algae found in South African formations 2.65 billion years old. From this time we can also date the first limestone concretions of the stromatolithic type. These are accumulations of diatom and algoid microfilaments around which photosynthesis deposits successive crusts.

The first unicellular plants formed the essence of the living world for most of the Precambrian era. Protected from ultraviolet rays by their aquatic life, these chlorophyllian organisms, in the course of more than a billion years, entirely transformed the terrestrial environment. Through photosynthesis, they freed enough oxygen to form an ozone screen in the high atmosphere, which could intercept ultraviolet rays, those of the longest wavelength which are most dangerous to life.

With this screen, life was able to gain in complexity and differentiation. A new and decisive stage was reached in the appearance of the first perfect cells, called eucaryota, possessing a differentiated nucleus. With this type of cell, the plant kingdom was able to develop and give birth to the animal kingdom.

Approximately 400 million years ago, when the free oxygen in the atmosphere reached 10 percent of its current level, life began to colonize the recently emerged continents. Then the first mosses and ferns made their appearance, closely followed by terrestrial invertebrates, then the first vertebrates with aerial respiration (fish with lobed fins and amphibians). Terrestrial life, whose great evolutionary stages were dominated by the emergence of reptiles (320 million years ago), mammals (190 million years ago), birds and the first flowering plants (130 million years ago), was from this point on to become widely differentiated.

The Times of Humanity

Primitive Man

Paleontology has made man discover two essential truths that are decisive for psychology: first, that he was created not in a single form nor from a single being, but, rather, as the result of evolutionary processes common to all other living species; and thus, that he is not immutable.

Man discovered the "naturalness" of his origins at the same time as his submission to the inexorable laws of mutation and natural selection. He rediscovered not long ago his total dependence on the environment, as well as his obligation to maintain vital relations with the physical and biological equilibria of the globe—relations which he had partially lost through excessive artificiality.

It is not easy to know when the human adventure began, so transitional does the passage between the first primates and *Homo sapiens* seem.

The time of what is properly termed "humanity" extends back around 3,300,000 years. In southern and eastern Africa, there appeared toward the end of the Tertiary period creatures with low foreheads, prominent eyebrow arches, and heavy jaws—the Australopithecans. Small but standing erect on their lower limbs, they already used rudimentary bone and stone tools for pounding, cutting, and scraping. These first hominoids were to be replaced by Pithecanthropans who appeared more than two million years ago. The latter still had many "primitive" traits: thick cranial bones and mandible, a receding forehead, prominent eyebrow arches, and a retracted chin. But their legs were long and straight, and their cranial capacity, far more developed than in Australopithecans, was almost equal to modern man's.

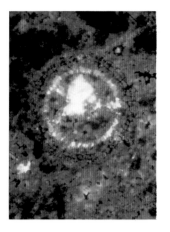

123

Radiolarians, micro-organisms with siliceous shells, appeared during the Precambrian and mark the beginning of the animal kingdom. Thecosphaera, shown here greatly enlarged and artificially colored, comes from the Carboniferous period of Montagne Noire, France.

124

These young Branchiosaurus petrolei, *from the Permian lagoons near Autun, France, belong to the amphibian line whose ancestors had conquered firm land 150 million years earlier.*

A social organization had already appeared among these hominoids who domesticated fire to cook their food. They gradually improved their tools, increasing the number of quartz artifacts and sculpting flints into rough "bifaces." The fabrication of these tools was a decisive factor in evolution. Henceforth, it comprised an "industry," transmitted through generations, which implies a communication of knowledge by language, the decisive vehicle of intelligence.

Having appeared in Africa, the Pithecanthropans spread across the globe, drawn by the conquest of new territories. We find them in North Africa, in Europe, China, and Java. These many lines of Pithecanthropans were succeeded about 1 million years ago by Neanderthal tribes. The Neanderthals were known primarily in Europe, but closely-related races developed in southeastern and northern Africa, in the Middle East, China, and in Indonesia. These men carved bone, and their stonework developed with the invention of special tools for each use. There were pointed ones worked in bifaces, scrapers, shavers, and cutting edges. With them the cult of the dead also emerged, as we know from the remains of their tombs.

Modern Man

The Neanderthals were the immediate predecessors of our own species, *Homo sapiens*, which appeared abruptly in Europe 37,000 years ago, and one of whose first races was Cro-Magnon Man. Henceforth there were to be no more early primitive types and the men living after this epoch are morphologically indistinguishable from contemporary man. Physically, they are no more different from us than are the present human races among themselves.

Homo sapiens gained the powers of conceptualization and aesthetic creativity. Thus art could develop (as we know from innumerable cave paintings discovered in Europe) at the same time that tools of flint, bone, and deerhorn were refined in a spectacular manner. At the end of the Ice Ages, 10,000 years ago, man gradually turned to agriculture and animal breeding. He renounced his nomadic life to found the first lakeside cities, and then villages with stone foundations. The Bronze Age was approaching and the great civilizations of antiquity were about to be born.

125

The contemporary of our human ancestors since the time of the first anthropomorpha, the Laurus nobilis, *appeared 10 million years ago. This specimen from the Pliocene epoch of Puy-de-Dôme, France, owes its color to ferric oxides.*

We cannot help but be struck by the acceleration of human evolution, one of whose distinctive traits seems to have been its exponential development: 30 million years since the appearance of the primates; 3,300,000 years since the first hominoids; 37,000 years since the entry of *Homo sapiens* onto the scene. The lifetime of individuals has also been considerably lengthened, passing from thirty years for Neanderthal man, to thirty-eight for Bronze Age man, to the current seventy years. In the same time, the population growth has followed a dizzying curve, moving from an estimated 125,000 individuals two million years ago to about one million 30,000 years ago, then to 87 million 8,000 years ago, to reach 1 billion around 1820, and soon to pass beyond 4 billion people.

Just how high can this curve rise, and what kinds of events does nature hold in store for the future of humanity? Paleontology alone cannot answer such questions, but the estimates it has still to confer on the rhythms of evolution can only confirm the unrest among demographers, economists, and ecologists.

126

A number of the coral reefs in southern oceans, which we appreciate today for their beauty, were already flourishing in the Tertiary period. Some still exist in Europe. An example is this Diploastrea diversiformis, *found in the Miocene epoch reefs of the Landes region in France.*

127
128

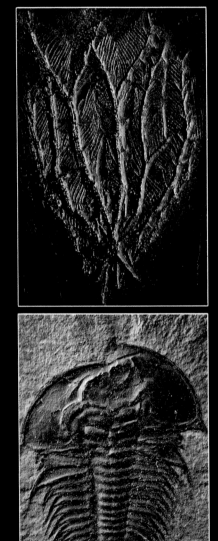

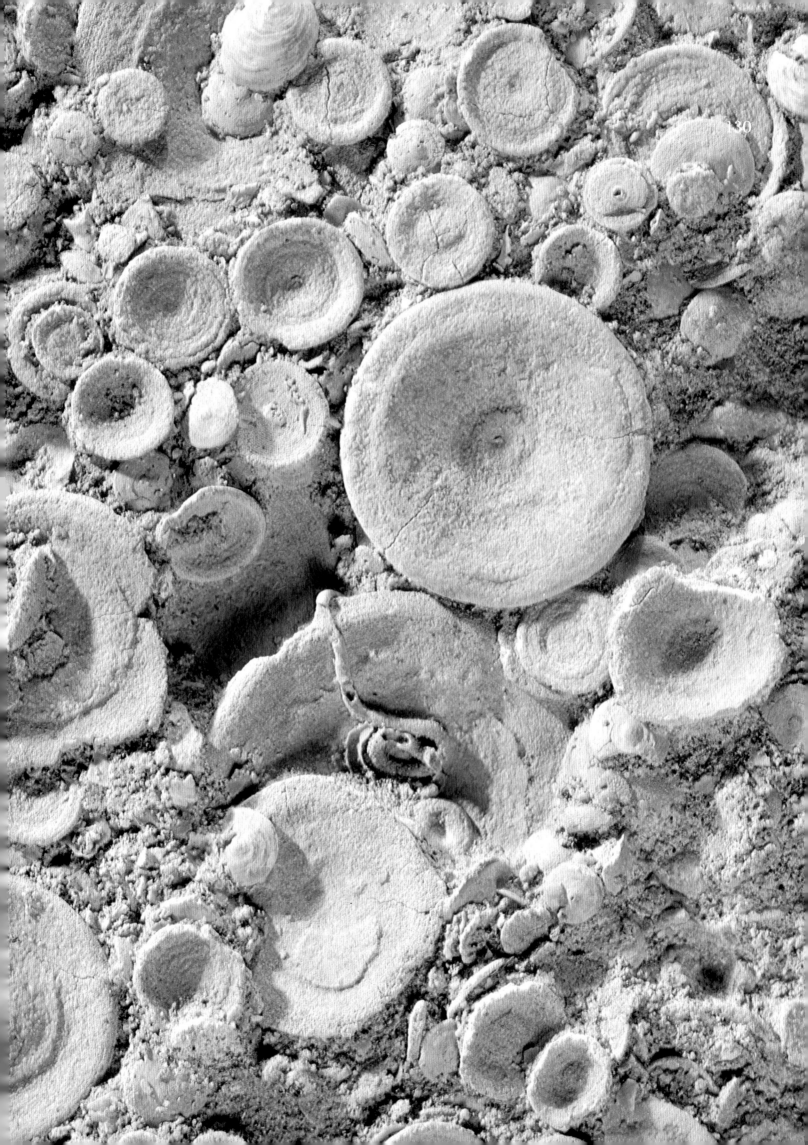

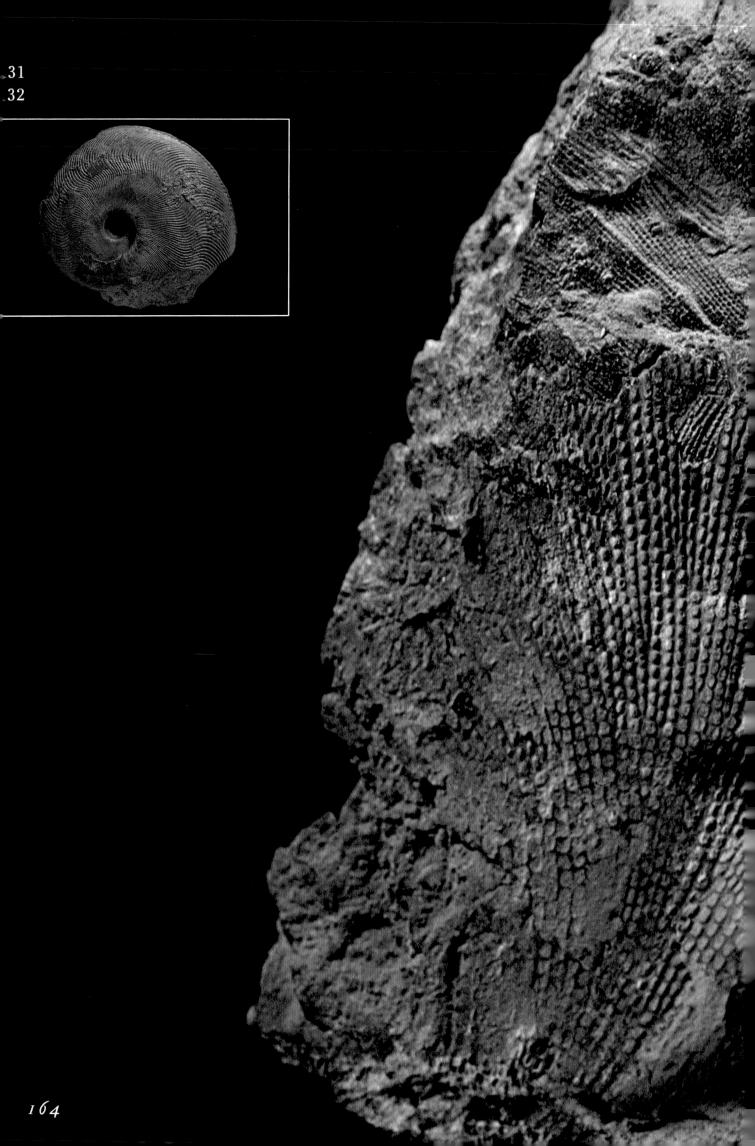

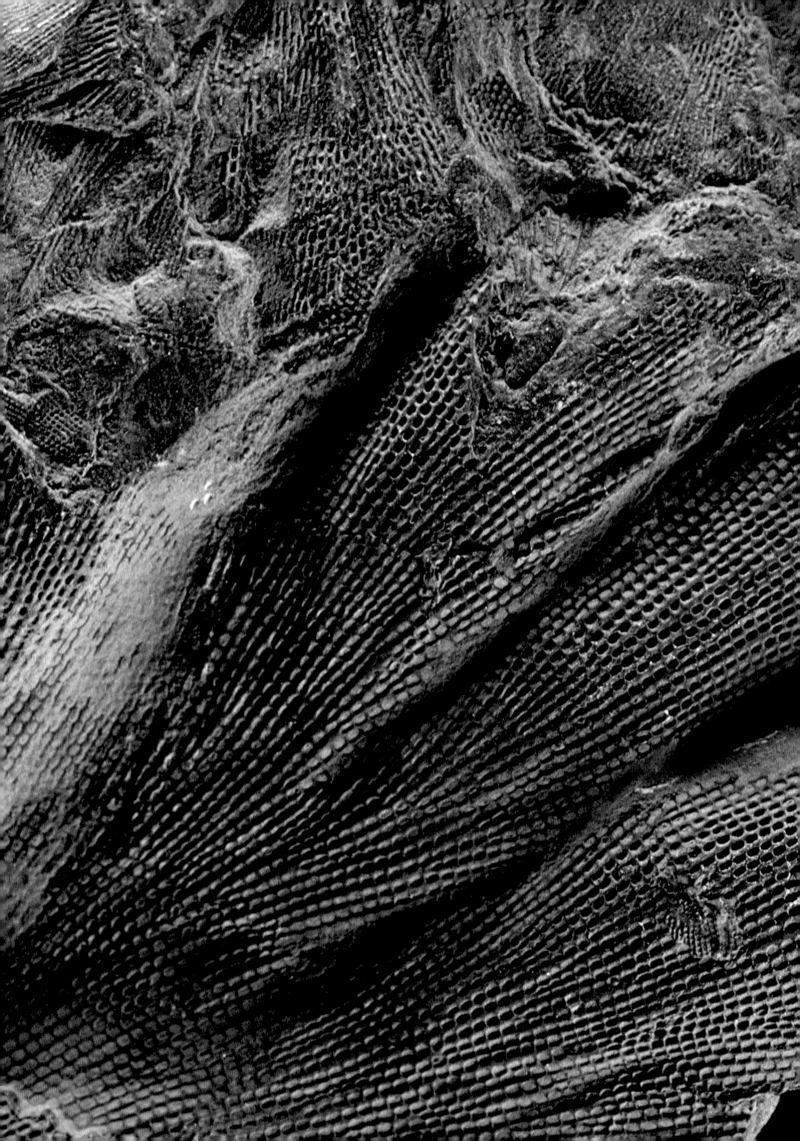

137

138

139

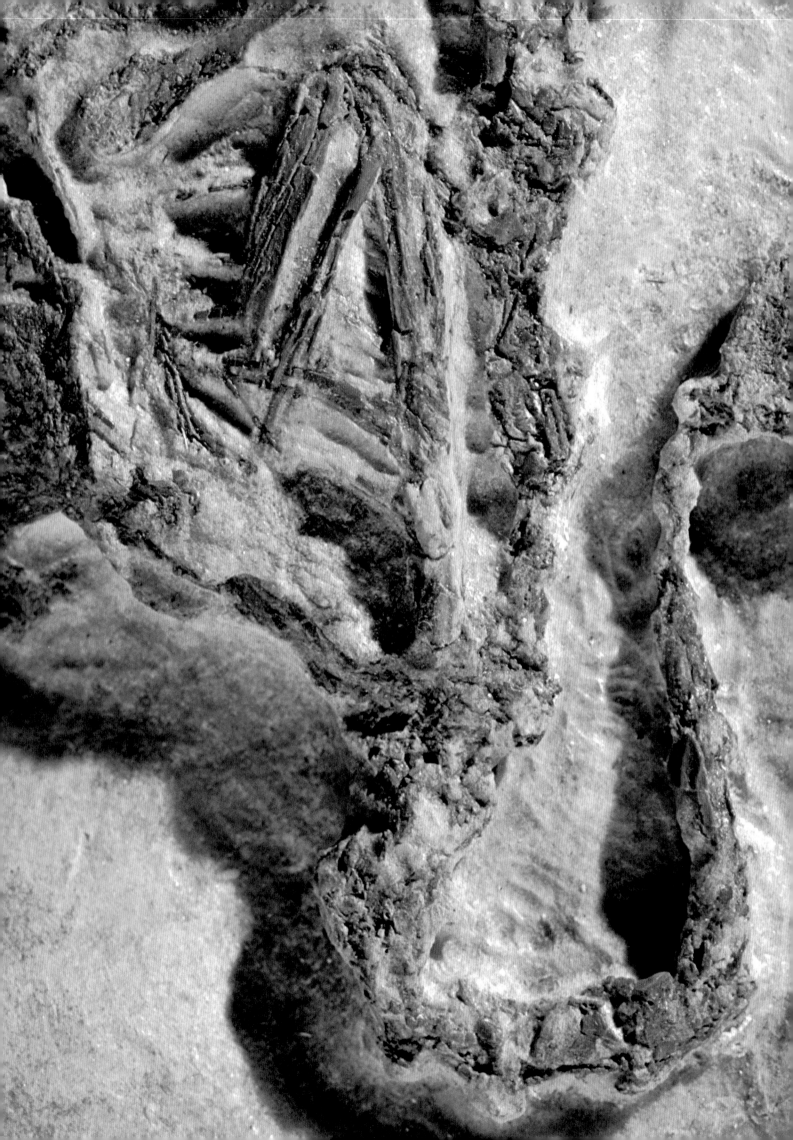

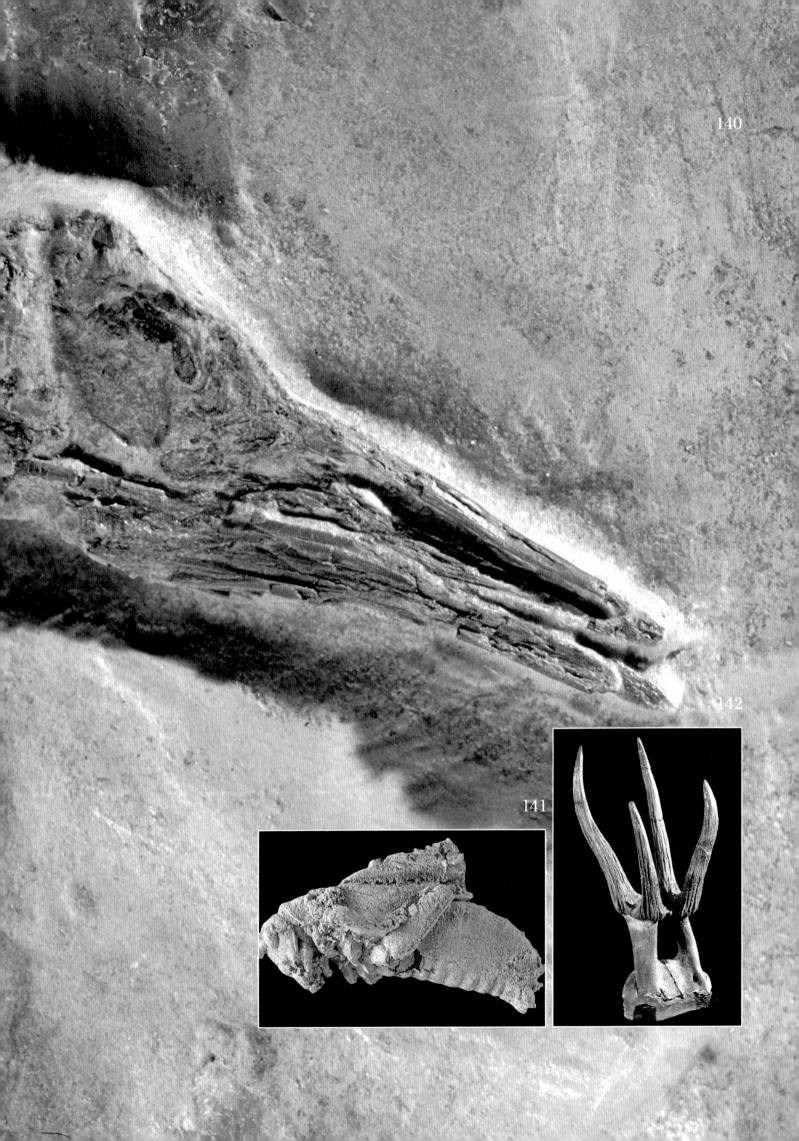

5. Epilogue

The fossil world is presently regarded as a world foreign to our own, a universe to which we are linked only by more or less accurate notions of unsoundable lengths of time, of evolution, and of biological and energetic heritage.

In vain the march of time teaches us that we live on the acquisitions of the past; with similar difficulty our present anthropocentrism forces us to admit the reality of an incomplete continuum, in which our human species represents only a tiny episode.

Yet it is clear that the evolution of the biosphere has not ended with man's arrival. It proceeds by fits and starts in which each transformation is both the result of past events and a prelude to the future. If the future cannot be analyzed, the great stages of the terrestrial past are, in contrast, increasingly well known. And the instructions gleaned from them can be used for the illumination of our present.

For more than 3 billion years an intensely vital activity has been developing on our planet with innumerable repercussions, and a development so intricate it cannot be wholly described. Here we must mention only the enrichment of the atmosphere by oxygen, and the screening out of noxious ultraviolet rays by ozone; the elaboration and concentration of many mineral substances; the mitigation and diversification of the terrestrial climate; the distribution of plant and animal populations; the constant adjustment of the many physico-chemical equilibria; the genesis and fixation of soils; and so on.

Whatever we may do, we are firmly fixed within this nature. Not only are we its biological emanation, we are economically dependent on it to the degree that our vital environment is tightly linked to biological fossil activity. From it flow the limestones, plasters, and cements we use for building, the phosphates that fertilize our soils, the coal and oil we burn, and many other primary materials for our industries.

These substances comprise what we call "unrenewable" natural resources—those requiring highly specific conditions for composition and, most important, considerable lapses of time. Tens of millions of years are required for their development, but tens of years alone are needed for human power to exhaust them. Twentieth-century man thoughtlessly consumes the fossil riches accumulated over the course of hundreds of millions of years. He tests his power and measures his luck. It remains for him to measure the risks.

If such knowledge incites us to economic prudence, this circumspection must finally give way to wonder before the profound and irresistable vital power by which the infinitely small, with the aid of time, can create the immeasurable. Neither judge nor reference nor master, man is inevitably integrated in an enormous living network. Let us hope that his intelligence allows him to better sound its complexity, his sensibility to appreciate its riches.

144

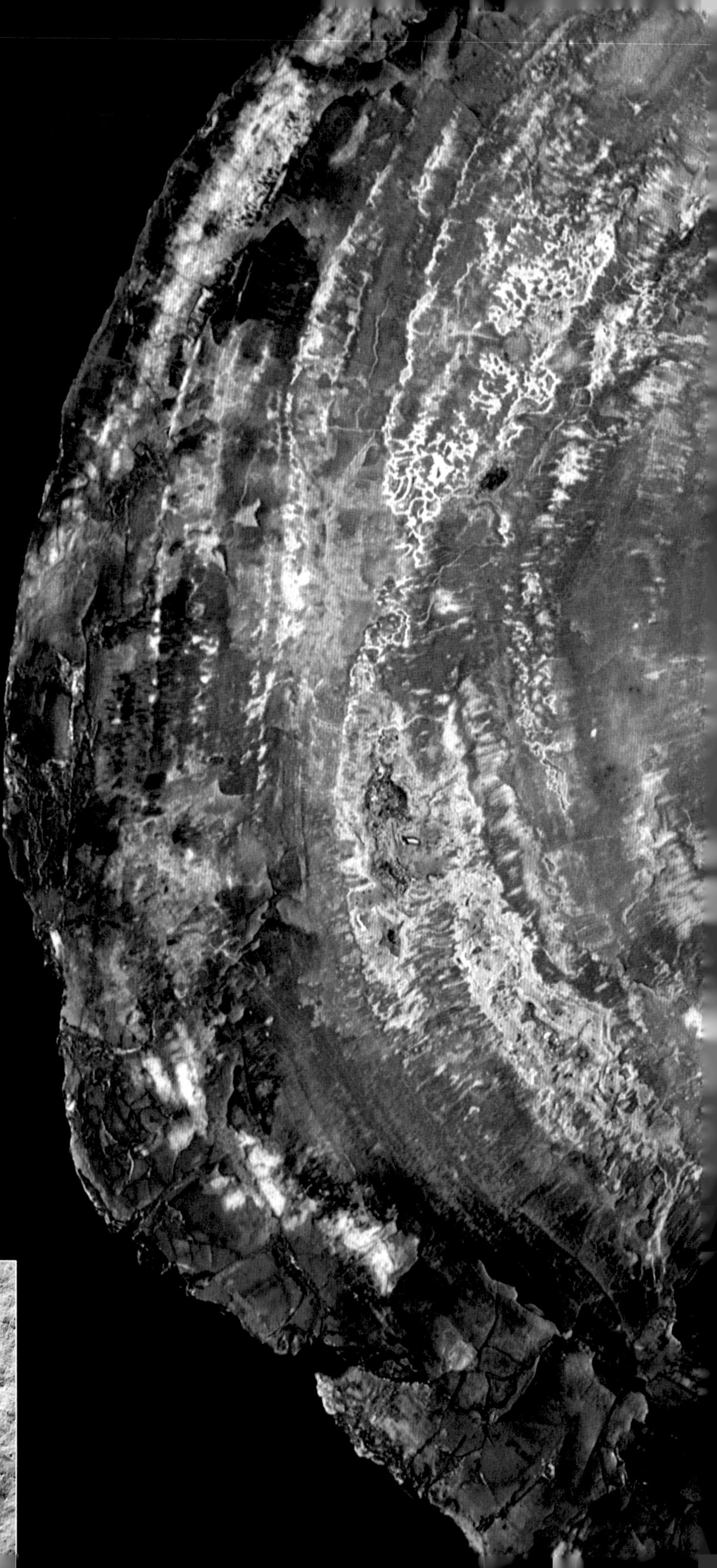

145

146

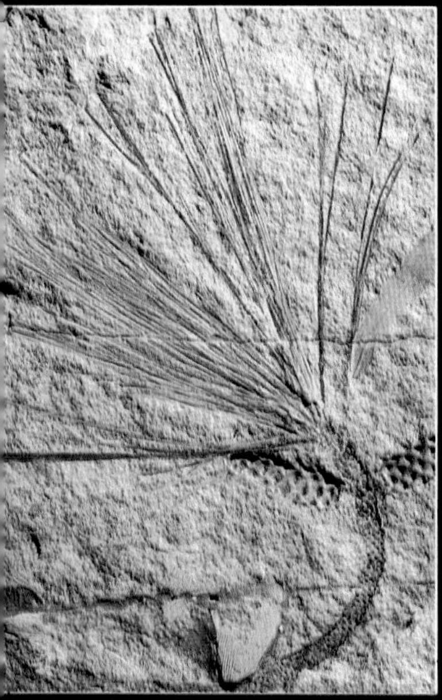

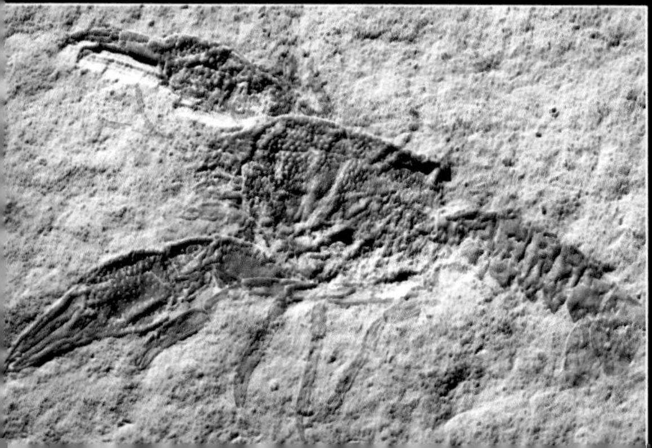

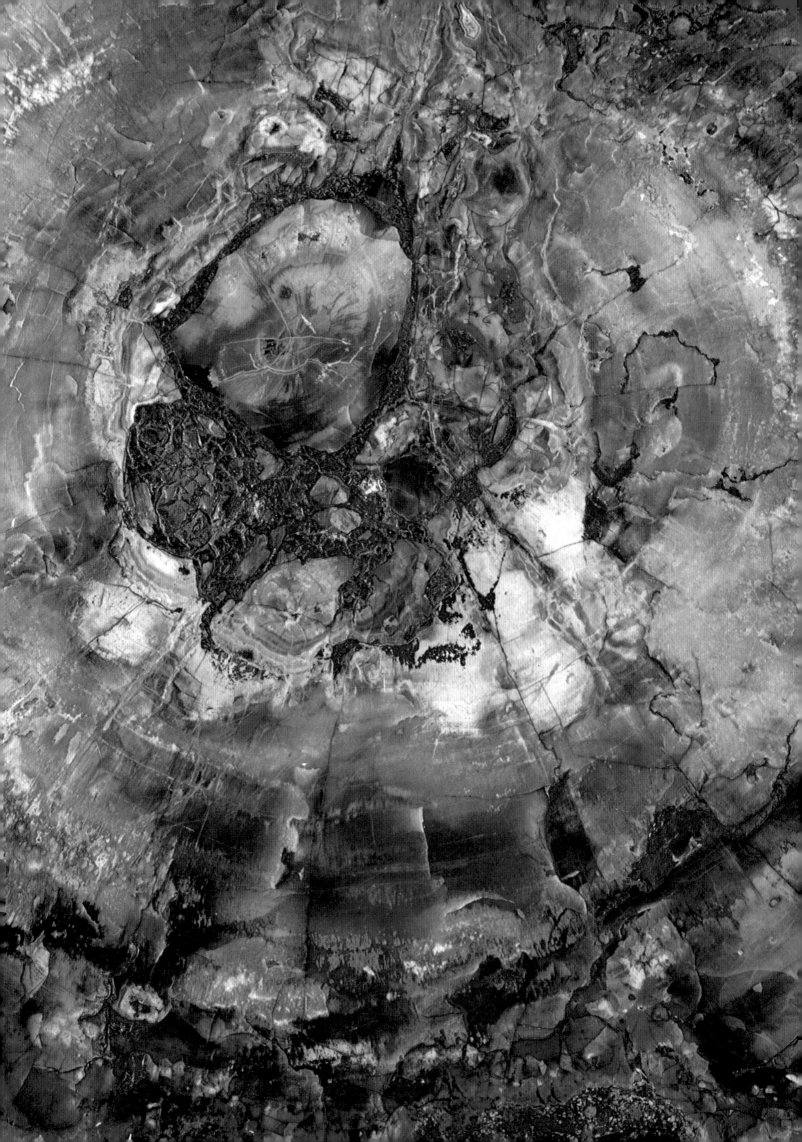

Appendices

149

Annotations to Color Plates

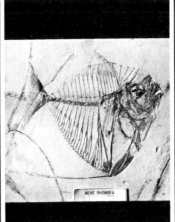

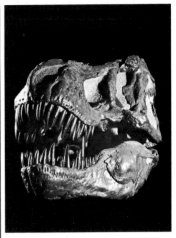

3

Clypeaster scillae, *a Miocene epoch echinoderm from Vence, France. The morphology of this remarkable species lets us appreciate the beauty of the petallike arrangement characteristic of the most highly evolved, irregular sea-urchins and unchanged by fossilization. Initially bearing short, thin spines like bristles, this species was accustomed to seek nutrition by digging in the slime of the ocean depths.*

4

Cosmoceras duncani, *a Middle Jurassic cephalopod from Calvados, France. The ammonites have always been among the most popular and symbolic of fossils. A characteristic shape based on a perfect logarithmic spiral, a wide variety of ornamentation, and their abundance make these cephalopods—now extinct— evocative witnesses to strange and distant eras.*

5

Mene rhombea, *an Upper Eocene fish from Monte Bolca, Italy. This site, worked for four centuries, has already furnished thousands of fish of extremely varied genera. Fifty million years of fossilization have preserved the perfection of their delicate skeletal architecture. Here nature attains the beauty of a deliberate work of art.*

6

Tyrannosaurus rex, *an Upper Cretaceous reptile from the United States. The largest and most fearsome of earthly carnivores, this dinosaur must have evoked terror all around him. Weighing eight to ten tons, standing ten meters long and five meters high, he had a monstrous jaw with teeth fifteen to twenty centimeters long. Only a few other reptiles, with their sharp horns and spiny, murderous scales, could resist him.*

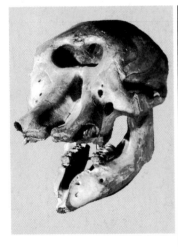

7

Mastodon americanus, *a Pleistocene epoch proboscidian from America. Famous for their size and remarkable tusks, mastodons lived throughout Europe, Asia, Africa, and America during the Tertiary and early Quaternary periods. An enormous nasal orifice and the strong roots of their tusks gave their exaggerated cranium the strange appearance of a mythological monster.*

8

Arsinotherium zittelli, *an Oligocene epoch mammal from Fayoum, Egypt. Three meters long and 1.75 meters tall, this strange quadruped is the sole representative of its type. It had a cranium curiously lengthened by two enormous nasal bones above a narrow muzzle. Its teeth made it a unique type of herbivore. Heavy and massive, it must have lived in the marshes.*

9

Promicroceras planicosta, *a Liassic cephalopod from Lyme Regis, England. The ammonites comprise one of the truly representative groups of our planet's biological past. They appeared about 400 million years ago at the start of the Devonian Period, and prospered up to the end of the Mesozoic era when, just like the dinosaurs, they disappeared for reasons that still evade us.*

22

Hornera striata, *Miocene epoch sea moss from Maine-et-Loire, France. Although found throughout sedimentary rocks from the beginning of the Ordovician period, bryozoa, small colonizing organisms, are generally little known among collectors, Through their accumulation, they have made large contributions to the formation of limestone sediments.*

23

Eryon arctiformis, *an Upper Jurassic arthropod from Solnhofen, Bavaria, Germany. Though known since the Lower Cambrian, the mostly aquatic group of crustaceans has evolved only slightly. Their chitinous carapace makes for good preservation, and they would certainly be more abundant in excavation sites had they not fallen to numerous predators.*

24

Dapalis minutus, *an Oligocene epoch fish from Aix-en-Provence, France. In the Oligocene epoch the region of Aix-en-Provence still enjoyed a subtropical climate and was occupied by a vast lake with seasonal variations in salt levels. These little fish abounded in it, since they were well adapted to its changes. To this day we find their fossil forms in marls sprinkled with gypsum deposits, accompanied by flora and fauna of incredible richness.*

25

A lamellibranch deposit from the Thyrenian period sea, found in Mers-el-Kébir, Algeria. The Thyrenian, the warm period in the Mediterranean Pleistocene, corresponds to a general elevation in sea levels. It was the last important change before our current epoch, when the cooler climate diminished the number of warm climate species. Glycymeris violacescens still exists in the Mediterranean.

26

A branch of Upper Oligocene Sequoia sternbergii (a conifer) from Styrie, Austria. Only two species of sequoia are still extant today, and both are found in California. But this genus, nevertheless, knew a great expansion during the Tertiary period throughout the temperate zone of the north American hemisphere, to Spitsberg and Alaska, which at that time enjoyed a far milder climate than it does today.

27

Lymnocardium syrmiense, *a lamellibranch from Boecin near Novi Sad, Hungary. During the Pliocene epoch, large inland seas with brackish waters (the remains of an ancient marine gulf) stretched over the center of Europe, much as the Caspian and Aral Seas do today. The fauna, which was abundant but poor in number of species represented, was largely restricted to cardium, which became the king of this enormous Pontocaspian domain.*

28

Pseudocidaris durandi, *from the Upper Jurassic of Dra-el-Ahmar, Algeria. Finding a fossilized regular sea urchin still armed with its spines is the rarest of events, since the spines fall off soon after the animal's death. Among cidaridae, which have populated reefy areas since their appearance in the Triassic period, these spines are remarkably developed and allow the urchin to move about.*

29

A group of Acrospirifer speciosus, *Devonian period brachiopods from the Sahara. The diversification of the terrestrial climate began only toward the end of the Paleozoic era. And, particularly during the Devonian period, a uniformly tropical temperature predominated throughout the world's shallow seas. This was the preferred milieu of the brachiopods, and during the Devonian and Silurian periods they took over all of the seas.*

30

Trigonia crenulata, *Middle Cretaceous lamellibranch from Mans, France. With rudist (other lamellibranches) and nerines (gastropods), the trigonia can be included among the most characteristic mollusks of the Mesozoic era. We frequently find them together in the same sites, on the periphery of coral reefs that had been hot, shallow waters.*

31

Imprint of Zamites epibius, an Oligocene epoch cycadophyte from the Vaucluse, France. These gymnosperms, direct descendents of the strange "seed ferns" (Pteridospermaphyta) of the Paleozoic era, still have very archaic characteristics. The palm-shaped fronds were arranged in a "bouquet" at the top of a trunk very like that of a palm tree. They lived in the midst of tropical flora including, among other plants, actual palm trees.

32

Limestone of Nummulites spira, an Eocene epoch foraminifera from Hindoustan. Interpreted for centuries as petrified coins, the nummulites are giant unicellular organisms that secrete a chalky, disc-shaped limestone shell, often exceeding ten centimeters. Sectioned like this specimen, the spiraling cells can easily be observed. The animal itself occupied the last section.

33, 34

Two specimens of Arcestes Galeiformis (cephalopod) dating from the end of the Triassic period in Salzburg and Hallstadt, Austria. The fine polish of these specimens indicates the many marbled joints corresponding to the

internal divisions separating the shell into cells, of which the animal occupied only the last one. The arcestes formed part of the highly articulated Alpine Triassic ammonites, which were true ends of the series, verging on extinction.

35

Pleurotomaria armata, Middle Jurassic period gastropod from Calvados, France. Pleurotomairs appeared in the Triassic period and experienced their maximum development in the Jurassic period. Several species linger in today's seas (near Antilles, Japan, and Indonesia) where they sought refuge at depths varying from 100 to 300 meters, while the Jurassic species inhabited shallow waters.

36

Douvilleiceras clementinum, Middle Cretaceous period cephalopod from Dieuville, Aube, France. Ammonites, and particularly those of the Cretaceous period, help us distinguish very precise stratigraphic horizons. Ornamented forms such as this one are characteristic of coastal areas, with smooth forms generally indicating deeper aspects.

37

Polished transversal section of Aulopora serpens, coral of the Middle Devonian from the Eifel Mountains, Germany. Formerly confused with a "flower whose leaves have opened out," this specimen, like all other corals, was classified in the plant kingdom until the eighteenth century. In 1850, they were still called "zoophytes" (animal-plants) due to the fact that many of them lived in branched chains fixed to marine floors.

38

Transverse section of a growth of Carboniferous Lepidodendron, a specimen lycopodium from Haute-Garonne, France. The lepidodendrons, an exclusively fossil group, are giant lycopods, some thirty meters high, which reigned throughout the Carboniferous period in continents still scattered with vast marshy stretches. The sturdy trunk ended in an ample crown of leafy branches that bore cones as fruit.

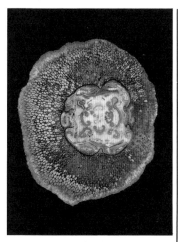

39

Transverse section of Psaronius Brasiliensis, a Permian fern from Piauhy, Brazil. The trunk of this arborescent fern was fairly slender and often reached ten meters in height. It was encircled by a casing of foliar stems much like the trunks of palm trees. The fronds and fruits are known under other names. Spectacular representatives of Paleozoic flora, they are today confined to the intertropical zone.

40

A winged ant (hymenopterous insect) enclosed in a fragment of Upper Eocene amber from the Baltic regions. Having made their appearance during the Liassic, ants in the Tertiary attained such a degree of development that few other insect families were comparable in number of individuals or species. More than 370 species of hymenoptera (bees, wasps, ants) have been identified in Baltic amber.

41

Homœosaurus jourdani, the latest Jurassic reptile from the Plan de Canjuers, Var, France. This small, lizardlike reptile belongs to the order of rhynchocephalia that appeared in the Triassic and underwent great expansion at the end of the Jurassic. Today their number has been so reduced that only a single survivor exists, the sphenodon, a singular reptile sixty centimeters long. It is a true "living fossil," inhabiting the islets neighboring New Zealand.

42

Pterodactylus, an Upper Jurassic flying reptile from Bavaria. The pterodactyls, pterosaurs from the Upper Jurassic and Cretaceous periods, make up several species whose length varies from that of a sparrow to that of an eagle. Their wings were formed by membranes supported on their fourth digits, and they were mediocre fliers, hovering near the coastlines in search of fish.

43

Marrolithus ornatus, Ordovician Period arthropod from Czechoslovakia. Trilobita were the main representatives of the arthropods throughout the Paleozoic and reached their apogee at the beginning of the Ordovician Period, but in the Permian Period they became totally extinct after a reign of 320 million years. This small species, which was very short and only 2.5 centimeters wide, was part of a well diversified group that has permitted an accurate definition of stratigraphic lines.

44

Spiropora elegans, Middle Jurassic Period sea moss from Calvados, France. Small marine animals called bryozoa are generally characteristic of shallow regions, where they formed colonies of various types. Despite its great fragility, this one was fossilized wholly intact, along with the organisms it lived with, in a region of algae and crinoid prairies.

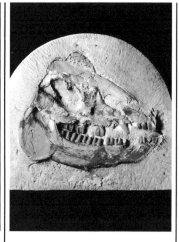

45

Palaeotherium curtum, a mammal from the gypsum beds of Montmartre in Paris, France. The study of the fossils at Montmartre was one of Cuvier's most important and famous endeavors. This Palaeotherium ("old animal") was one of those that permitted the naturalist to pursue his anatomy studies and attempt his reconstructions. Later the gypsum beds of Vitry yielded a complete skeleton, now in the Museum of Paris.

46

Mosasaurus Hoffmanni, an Upper Cretaceous reptile from Maestricht, the Netherlands. Known from 1870 on by this enormous head and described by Cuvier, in a classic memoir, under the name "The Great Animal of Maestricht," the mosasaurs are gigantic carnivorous marine reptiles with members transformed into fins. A richly diversified group, they lived in the seas of the Upper Cretaceous Period. Though they often exceeded ten meters in length, they had many affinities with lizards.

47

Silicified limestone containing Potamides lapidum, an Eocene epoch gastropod from around Paris. During the Eocene epoch, the Paris basin was filled by a vast lagoon-sea gulf bordered by lacustrine zones. Numerous cerithians, of which this species was one, grew in these areas. They formed layers of shelly limestone, often silicified as here, side by side with marly layers and gypsum deposits several meters deep.

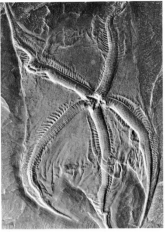

48–67

Loriolaster mirabilis *and* Ophiura primigenia, *Lower Devonian period echinoderms from Bundenbach, Germany. Ophiuroids, close relatives of starfish, appeared in the Lower Ordovician and endure to this day, when it is not uncommon to encounter them under stones at low tide. In the Lower Devonian, much of*

western Europe was covered by a warm sea with deposits of fine silts (today slate). These slates permitted the preservation of many fossil echinoderms (crinoids and asteroids) down to their smallest details, presenting striking images of life at the depths of a sea 400 million years old.

66

Populus transversa, a Miocene angiosperm from Oeningen, Germany. Pressed between two sedimentary layers like the leaves of a book, this 20-million-year-old poplar leaf has retained all the delicacy of its veins and part of its cuticle. Like most deciduous trees in today's forests, the poplar made its first appearance in the Lower Cretaceous.

68

Synastrea geometrica, an Upper Cretaceous coral from Maestricht, the Netherlands. Such colonial coral made few contributions to Jurassic and Cretaceous coral reefs, since they preferred quieter waters. The specimen presented here is an "internal cast"; the coral skeleton was dissolved during fossilization and only its filling of hardened limestone silt remains.

69

Aeger insignis, an Upper Jurassic decapod crustacean from Solnhofen, Bavaria. Shrimp, which emerged in the Triassic period, but are rare in the fossil state, are nevertheless common to the lithographic stones of Solnhofen, a site noted for its perfect preservation of many crustaceans with chitinous shells. This fine example is five centimeters long and has all its appendages firmly connected.

70

Dickinsonia costata, an enigmatic Precambrian fossil from Ediacara, Australia. This 700-million-year-old specimen is one of the oldest and best preserved fossil animals of this length (6.5 centimeters). We can interpret it as the imprint of a protomedusa, a group whose traces are found in the same site. The original is at the University of Adelaide, Australia.

71

Limestone containing archaeocyathids from the Lower Cambrian in Mongolia. Archaeocyathids are spongelike organisms from the Cambrian period with a remarkably structured skeleton, whose smallest details are preserved to this day. An acid bath has permitted us to see all the delicacy of this specimen, more than 570 million years old.

72

A natural cast of the internal cavity of a Miocene Clypeaster (echinoderm) from Malta Clypeasters, irregular sea urchins appearing in the Eocene epoch, are abundant in the sandy Miocene regions where they serve as excellent stratigraphic "indicators." This specimen's shell was dissolved during fossilization, and the internal cavity shown here filled up with silica.

73

"Mummified" Oligocene frog from the phosphorites of Quercy, France. The contents of swallow holes and grottoes from the Oligocene epoch form the important phosphite sites at Quercy. They were found to contain a plentiful and largely cave-dwelling animal life, which is famous both for its opulence and for the astonishing number of its specimens. One of these is this frog, a veritable mummy made of 35-million-year-old calcium phosphate.

74

Examples of pyritous fossils. The chemical components of organisms, and often their gangue, are generally transformed in the course of fossilization. Thus, we find fossils made of a variety of substances: crystalline calcite, sulphurs of iron or copper, hematitite, gypsum, and silica. The crystalline pyrites covering these small ammonites interpret the very specific conditions of fossilization as a highly reduced environment.

75

Pecten Quadricostatus, Upper Cretaceous lamellibranches from Maestricht, the Netherlands. Preserved in its original colors in hardened sand from the old North Sea, this 70-million-year-old scallop shell is not much different from those we find today on the sandy banks of seashores. These pectens first appeared in the Triassic period, but have evolved very little up to the present.

76

Flabellaria lamanonis, a monocotyledonous angiosperm from the Upper Oligocene in Aix-en-Provence, France. Fossil monocotyledons are rare finds. This now extinct genus is related to today's palm trees. Its neighbors were dracena, magnolias, mimosas, and camphor trees, the elements of a flora still dominant in Europe during the Oligocene epoch, though deciduous trees were gradually beginning to take over.

77

Neritoma ponderosa, Middle Jurassic gastropod from Martigny, Aisne, France. We can still admire the colored marks of the original decoration on this 160-million-year-old shell. Many examples of fossil mollusks (and some even from the Paleozoic era) are preserved in their original tones.

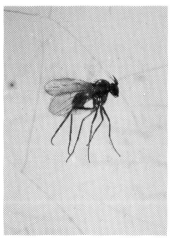

78, 79

Blocks of Baltic amber dating from the Oligocene epoch and containing two-winged insects. The true origin of amber—a fossil resin flowing from different types of conifers—was guessed at during antiquity. Although amber deposits were found throughout the world from the Carboniferous period to the Pleistocene epoch, the most abundant and famous amber comes from the northern regions of Europe. These zones, which were inundated in the early Tertiary, saw the emergence of a large island covered with resinous forests during the Lower Eocene. The amber contained in layers of clay may have been uprooted and transported far away by the thawing of glaciers or by the sea. At first collected on the shoreline, amber was later extracted from mines and quarries. It was initially sought by collectors and artists, but it now interests scientific minds because of its composition and its rich harvest of entrapped insects.

80

An insect trapped in a block of Baltic Oligocene amber. The remarkable diversification of insects is linked to the emergence of flowering plants. Since insects are rarely fossilized, due to their delicacy, their enclosure in amber has allowed preservation of numerous specimens. Study of the entomological fauna in Baltic amber provides a fairly accurate reconstruction of the milieu and biological conditions prevailing in northern Europe at the time.

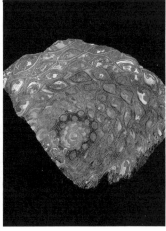

81

Transversal section cut in the stem of a Thamnopteris (arborescent fern) from the Australian Permian period. This thin section, photographed in transparency, shows the scars left in the stem by the insertion of stalks. The group to which thamnopteris belongs still exists today as the sole line of fossils descending from such an ancient past.

82

Bird feathers from the Upper Oligocene from Saint-Gérand-le-Puy, Allier, France. The fragility of bird remains makes them unsuitable objects for preservation, and discovery of such remains has been limited to a small number of exceptional sites. Saint-Gérand-le-Puy has given us not only bones but also eggs and feathers, in a remarkable state of preservation despite their 26 million years.

83

Pulchellis galeata, a Lower Cretaceous cephalopod from Villa de Leiva, Boyaca Province, Colombia. This specimen owes its ebony tint to the many ferrous elements in it. Its hard silicified gangue has also retained the perfect polish of its living form. This is one of the most characteristic genera of the end of the Lower Cretaceous period in northern Europe and America.

84

Head of Metoposaurus ouazzoui, an Upper Triassic stegocephalian from Atlas, Morocco. The first inhabitants of the Devonian forests, stegocephalians existed until the Jurassic period. During the Triassic, they expanded into giant forms with a characteristic large, heavy cranium. Metoposaurs often reached a length of 2.5 meters and fed on the fish of the swamps he lived in. One Moroccan site has furnished the remains of more than seventy specimens.

85

Diplomystus brevissimus, a bony Middle Cretaceous fish from Hakel, Lebanon. Found pressed between two hard calcite beds, this ten-centimeter-long fish was a member of a rich fauna that populated the Tethys (ancient Mediterranean), then still open to the Orient and shallow at the shoreline. The site of Hakel is known for its abundant, finely preserved fossils and has given us many mollusks, echinoderms, and crustaceans.

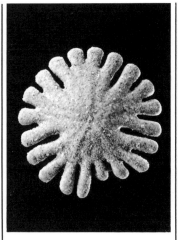

86

Rotula orbiculus, an Upper Pliocene echinoderm from Porto-Alexander, Angola. Scutellaria, irregular sea urchins that emerged in the Eocene, have remarkable flat, disc-shaped forms and slits, holes, and apertures characteristic of all the different genera in this family. Through their basic characteristics they are related to shield urchins and are ranked among the most highly evolved of sea urchins.

97

Garniericeras catenulatum, an Upper Jurassic cephalopod from the Moscow region. Light playing over the microscopic aragonite sheets of such shells creates the pearly shimmer still visible on many fossil specimens. Such luminosity, emphasized by the structure of the sutures, gives this small Jurassic ammonite its beauty.

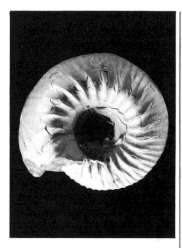

98

Cadoceras elatmae, *a Middle Jurassic cephalopod from Elatma, Soviet Union. The famous Elatma site contains a rich fauna composed of lamellibranches, gastropods, and cephalopods that, because of the exceptional conditions of the site, have preserved their original luster after 155 million years.*

99

Calymene nigarensis, *Lower Silurian arthropod from Ohio. We rarely encounter fossils in characteristic poses. Calymene are an exception to this general rule, because trilobites are frequently wound up like sea-lice and fossilized in characteristic attitudes of defense. These are excellent stratigraphic fossils that are often found pyritized like the inhabitants of many shaley regions.*

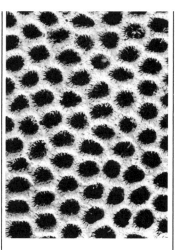

100

Calyxed surface of Favites, *a Neocene (recent Tertiary) coral from Suez. Since the Jurassic, favids have played a large part in building coral reefs, and many examples are found today throughout the Indo-Pacific province. We see them frequently in reefs from the Red Sea, which span the ages from the Miocene to the present. These calyxes are generally about five millimeters wide.*

101

Codiacrinus schultzei, *Lower Devonian echinoderm from Bundenbach, Germany. Bundenbach has presented us with quantities of echinoderms (mostly crinoids and stelleroids) that have been well preserved in slate clays corresponding to beds of fine, compressed mud. The striking pose of this crinoid was formed by the currents intermittently sweeping over the ocean floors.*

102

Saccocoma pectinata, *an Upper Jurassic echinoderm from Solnhofen, Bavaria. The genus* Saccocoma *contains the comatulae, crinoids that are either stemless or have lost their stems in adulthood, and float freely in the open seas. Comatulae appeared sometime in the Liassic epoch and have since expanded throughout the waters of the globe.*

103

Limestone *with crinoids, originating in the Lower Carboniferous of Colomb-Béchar, Algeria. Here we see the remains of an old crinoid "prairie" in which only fragments of stems still exist. Some are visible in cross-section, so that we can clearly see the path of the axial canal. Deposits almost wholly formed of crinoid fragments—called encrinal limestones—are particularly common to Jurassic sites.*

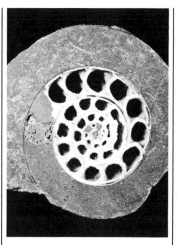

104

Section of an Upper Jurassic *Perisphinctes plicatilis from Calvados, France. This section cut into the shell's symmetrical structure shows the perfect logarithmic curve created by its winding. Ammonites and nautiloids secrete a series of cells in the course of their development, only to abandon them one after the other and use them for floats.*

105

Sassafras cretaceum, *an Upper Cretaceous angiosperm from Kansas. One of the major events at the beginning of the Cretaceous period was the development of angiosperms, true flowering plants that spread throughout Europe, Asia, and America with astonishing speed. The family of Lauraceae to which Sassafras belongs was already well established by the Upper Cretaceous period. This leaf, a fossil type of a still extant genus, has preserved intact the marks of its veining.*

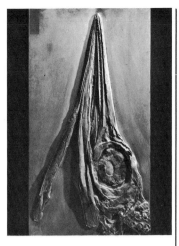

106

Stenopterygius crassico-status, *Liassic ichthyosaurus from Holzmaden, Wurtemberg, Germany. From the Triassic to the end of the Cretaceous periods, the oceans were populated by marine reptiles like the ichthyosaurus. Everything in these animals' structure (which was generally about three meters long) was designed for swimming, and their members resemble strong oars. The head of these strange fossils ends in a pointed, toothy muzzle much like the swordfish's.*

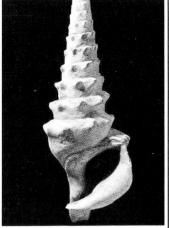

107

Campanila Giganteum, *Eocene epoch gastropod from the Oise, France. The largest specimens of cerethids can reach fifty-five centimeters in height, placing them among the largest gastropods of all time. Widely sought by collectors, they are undoubtedly the most famous of the Tertiary shells found in the Paris region. The huge shell functioned as a support for the many organisms that became attached to or lived on it.*

108

Phyllochilus polypora, *Upper Jurassic gastropod from Meuse, France. "Winged shells" is another name for these gastropods which, in their final stages of growth, secrete shell enlargements accompanied by "digits" or "veins" that make them veritable jewels. This one, still encrusted in a limestone matrix, has a wing-shaped growth eight centimeters high and marked by eleven streamlined digits.*

109

Stenopterygius quadriscissus, *a Liassic ichthyosaurus from Holzmaden, Wurtemberg, Germany. The Holzmaden beds are among the most fertile in ichthyosaurs. Thanks to remarkable fossilization in shales, we can often find the imprint of the skin encircling the related skeleton. It is even possible to identify within these animals ingested food and perhaps embryos, which would make ichthyosaurs viviparous reptiles.*

110

Seymouria, *Upper Carboniferous amphibians from Texas. Situated between stegocephalians (primitive amphibians) and the first reptiles, this 60-centimeter-long animal lived 290 million years ago in coal-bearing lagoons where it led an amphibian way of life. Fossilization preserved it in its last position, just as it had deposited itself on the floor of a muddy hole. (The original is in the Smithsonian Institution, Washington, D.C.)*

111

Lytoceras cornucopiae, *an Upper Liassic cephalopod from La Verpillière, Isère, France. This ammonite is fifteen centimeters in diameter and owes its brown-red color to the many iron oxides that filled it during fossilization. The size of ammonites varies according to genera and species from 1.0 centimeter to 2.5 meters, the record attained by Pachydiscus in the Upper Cretaceous period.*

112

Isophlebia aspasia, *an Upper Jurassic period insect (arthropod) from Solnhofen, Bavaria. While the giant Meganeura (65-centimeter wingspread) from the Paleozoic were not true dragonflies, these developed from the Liassic onward with a more modest but still fairly large form. This one has a wingspread measuring fifteen centimeters. In the Liassic, these insects also showed a preference for watery areas and swampy vegetation.*

113

Mesolimulus walchi, *an Upper Jurassic arthropod from Solnhofen, Bavaria. Dragonflies, which originated in the Permian, have developed very little throughout geological time. The species living in today's seas—true living fossils—are similar to those of the Paleozoic era and even closer to those of the Mesozoic, being differentiated largely by a heavier body.*

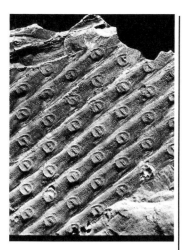

114

Sigillaria notata, *Carboniferous lycopod from Sarrebrück, Germany.* Sigillaria *were arborescent lycopods ten to twenty meters tall, with trunks often one meter in diameter. They formed a characteristic element of the coal-producing flora filling the forests from the Carboniferous to the Permian periods. Falling leaves left scars or "cushions" characteristic of the foliage, whose variations have been used to differentiate genera and species. The organs underground are known by the name Stigmaria.*

127

Agriocrinus inermis, *Lower Devonian echinoderm from Bundenbach, Rhenanie, Germany. The great variety of crinoids in Paleozoic and Mesozoic seas reflects multiple adaptations to diverse environments: while forms from reefy areas were thick and solidly constructed so as to resist disturbance by the movement of water, those from calmer depths—as at Bundenbach—present a fine, delicately honed architecture.*

128

Olenellus vermontanus, *a Lower Cambrian arthropod from Georgia, Vermont. Olenellids, specific to the Lower Cambrian, are among the most primitive of trilobites. Each of the eighteen genera of this well-diversified family was confined to a biogeographical province. The genus Olenellus spread over North America, Greenland, and Scotland; others were specific to Siberia, the Scandinavian and Baltic regions, and Morocco.*

129

Monophyllites Simonyi, *an Upper Triassic cephalopod from Hallstadt, Austria. During the course of development, the seams corresponding to the insertion of internal divisions on the shell's periphery became increasingly complicated. In the Paleozoic, they were simple in their winding. But by the Triassic, several genera had become uniquely contorted and were to achieve an astonishing level of complexity during the Jurassic and particularly at the end of the Cretaceous period.*

130

Orbitolina concava, *a Middle Cretaceous foraminifera from the Orne region, France. Though abundant in the Lower and Middle Cretaceous, orbitolina never lived until the Upper Cretaceous. They were widespread in the intertropical seas, living in dense populations on the salty floors. Several species, like the one shown here, were six centimeters in diameter.*

131

Fenestella membranacea, *a Carboniferous sea moss from Colomb-Béchard, Algeria. High magnification is required to appreciate the striking architecture of these tiny organisms, the builders of finely chiseled colonies in which each cell forms an individual dwelling. The architecture of the fenestellids, a purely Paleozoic group, is among the simplest yet most beautiful left by bryozoa.*

132

Harpoceras subplanatum, *from the Upper Liassic of La Verpillière, France. The hulls, straight or curving sides, tubers of varied forms and dimensions, and the frequently long spines decorating the shells of numerous ammonites (which we rely on to distinguish genera and species) fuse with characteristic joints and windings to direct the general classification of several thousand known forms.*

133

Salix, *a Tertiary angiosperm from Washington. Silicification permits the perfect preservation of structures. Hence, this transversal section of a willow tree, silicified and converted to pure agate on its periphery, shows the growth rings of the tree. Spring wood rings are represented by thin striations, while autumnal ones are heavy, providing tangible proof of seasonal variations identical to those of the present.*

134

Virgatites virgatus, *an Upper Jurassic cephalopod from the Moscow region. During the Upper Jurassic, as in numerous other times throughout the earth's history, the eastern Mediterranean was linked to the Arctic Ocean by a large stretch of water with a north-south orientation that submerged the central Russian plains. This inundation brought with it a northern fauna characterized by the lamellibranch* Buchia *and numerous ammonites, of which this is one species.*

135

Lumachelle with Monotis salinaria (lamellibranch) from the Upper Cretaceous in Hallstadt, Austria. The Triassic genus Monotis *was widespread throughout the eastern Mediterranean, Indonesia, Japan, Southern Australia, and the Arcto-Pacific region as far as California. It gave birth to many formal variations;* Monotis salinaria *is specific to the Alpine region.*

136

Otozamites, *a gymnosperm cycadophyte from the Upper Jurassic of Verona, Italy. The cycadophytes originated in the Triassic, and though they exist today, they are in decline.* Otozamites *has been interpreted as a leafy branch of* Williamsonia, *a cycadophyte belonging to the benetittales group that flourished from the Jurassic period to the Lower Cretaceous and is still extant. Its large fronds with small round pinnules could reach three meters in length.*

137

Myrsina umbellata, *a Pliocene angiosperm from Ouriçanga, Brazil. Expansion by angiosperms saw the decline of the gymnosperms. After the middle of the Cretaceous period, the flora took on its current appearance, and no important changes occurred in the Pliocene.* Myrsinala *are small trees, seven meters in height, that are extant today in the tropics. The beauty of this specimen is due to the tinting of its leaves by natural oxides.*

138

"Flower" of Williamsonia gigas, *a gymnosperm from the Jurassic period in Saltwick, England. Extending throughout the world, the genus* Williamsonia *itself made up the two tiers of Jurassic cycadophyte. This plant had a long trunk and was covered with leaves. Its reproductive organs were arranged in "flowers" quite different from those of angiosperms: they appeared on the trunk at the leaves' axil, and could be more than eleven centimeters in diameter.*

139

Isophlebia aspasia, *an Upper Jurassic insect (arthropod) from Solnhofen, Bavaria. During the Jurassic period the famous Solnhofen site, which has provided so many fossils in marvelous states of preservation, was a vast stretch of calm waters, quite shallow and warm—a sort of immense lagoon filled with life in which fine limestone silts (lithographic limestone) were deposited.*

140

Palaeortyx, *an Upper Eocene bird from the Montmartre gypsum in Paris. During the Upper Eocene epoch, the Paris basin was covered by vast evaporating lagoons, whose deposits today provide layers of gypsum. Cuvier systematically excavated them, uncovering a fauna rich in terrestrial and aquatic vertebrates, such as these birds. The order of rails, terrestrial running birds, first appeared in Europe in the Eocene and is today dispersed throughout the globe.*

141

Oligocene locust from the phosphorites of Quercy, France. The stunning phosphorite beds at Quercy provide us with innumerable insect remains—faithfully preserved due to specific mineralization—as well as many current vertebral forms. Here we find a harvest of beetles, termites, ants, locusts, and even fly pupae and larvae, completely petrified by the calcium phosphate.

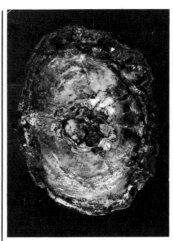

142

Dicrocerus elegans, *Miocene period mammalian cervidae from the site of Sansan, Gers, France. The Miocene saw the height of the mammalian expansion in the savannahs and subtropical forests. The first Oligocene cervidae had no antlers; after forms with persistent antlers, cervidae with deciduous antlers—such as Dicrocerus—made their appearance in the Miocene epoch. Deer, roe-deer, and elaphic stags date from Pliocene times. Along with the megacerous stag and reindeer, they formed prehistoric man's game.*

143

Emericeras, *a Lower Cretaceous cephalopod from Villa de Leiva. Colombia. Originating in the Lower Devonian in forms much like the orthocerus, ammoniters quickly adopted the rolled up shape that reduces the weight of their shell while insuring greater mobility. But their decline began with the Cretaceous period, and many took on strange and often surprising forms—like disjointed, "unwound," turreted, or crooked spirals, as well as some that were wholly irregular.*

144

A section of the trunk of a silicified Triassic resinous tree from Chalcedony Park, Arizona. More than 200 million years ago, what is today Arizona contained a large forest of resinous trees— perhaps the amancarian pines–whose petrified trunks, now fully transformed into jasper, are still strewn over the soil. The Indians took them for the bones of a giant monster or the broken weapons left over from a battle between giants and gods, and they were not exaggerating: the diameter of these trunks often exceeds one meter.

145

Pinus resurgens, *an Oligocene conifer (gymnosperm) from Armissan, Aube, France. The conifers, which are responsible for amber, first appeared in the Permian period, fanning out to their maximum expansion during the Jurassic. From the beginning they dominated the Northern hemisphere, just as the pine family does today. Here the delicate fossilization makes visible the female fruit under the needles.*

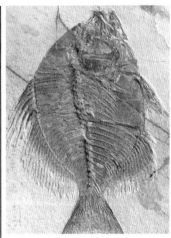

146

Eryma modestiformis, *an Upper Jurassic arthropod from Solnhofen, Bavaria. This small crustacean belongs to a family first known from Triassic times and that disappeared without descendents in the Upper Cretaceous. It was a walking animal related to the ancestors of crayfish and lobsters, equipped with two well developed globular pincers. It inhabited the waters of Europe and has been found as far away as Lebanon, Madagascar, Polynesia, and North America.*

147

Surface of a sea bottom from the Middle Cretaceous around Dieuville, Aube, France. With such a specimen we can easily reconstruct the composition of a fauna dwelling 115 million years ago in calm waters on shallow sandbanks: alongside ammonites (Hoplites interruptus) were lamellibranches, gastropods, and scaphopods (Dentalium decassatum), and several corals not in reef form (Trochocyathus conulus).

148

Pebble of black pyritized sandstone with mollusks from the Middle Cretaceous in England. This pebble, resulting when the sea dislodged fossil-bearing limes from a clay bank, contains a great variety of mollusks (lamellibranches, gastropods, and small ammonites) with several pyrite crystals glimmering among them. It is a beautiful object, but one of little scientific interest since there is no way of knowing its exact origin.

149

Archaephippus asper, *an Upper Eocene fish from Monte Balca, Italy. The beauty of the fish from Monte Balca amazed the first naturalists to study them. To find in Italian soil forms recalling those from the Chinese seas, the Indian Ocean, or the Antilles Sea seems inexplicable to those not guessing the truth of life's evolution and the vast length of geological time, which only the deepening of paleontological science can reveal.*

Table

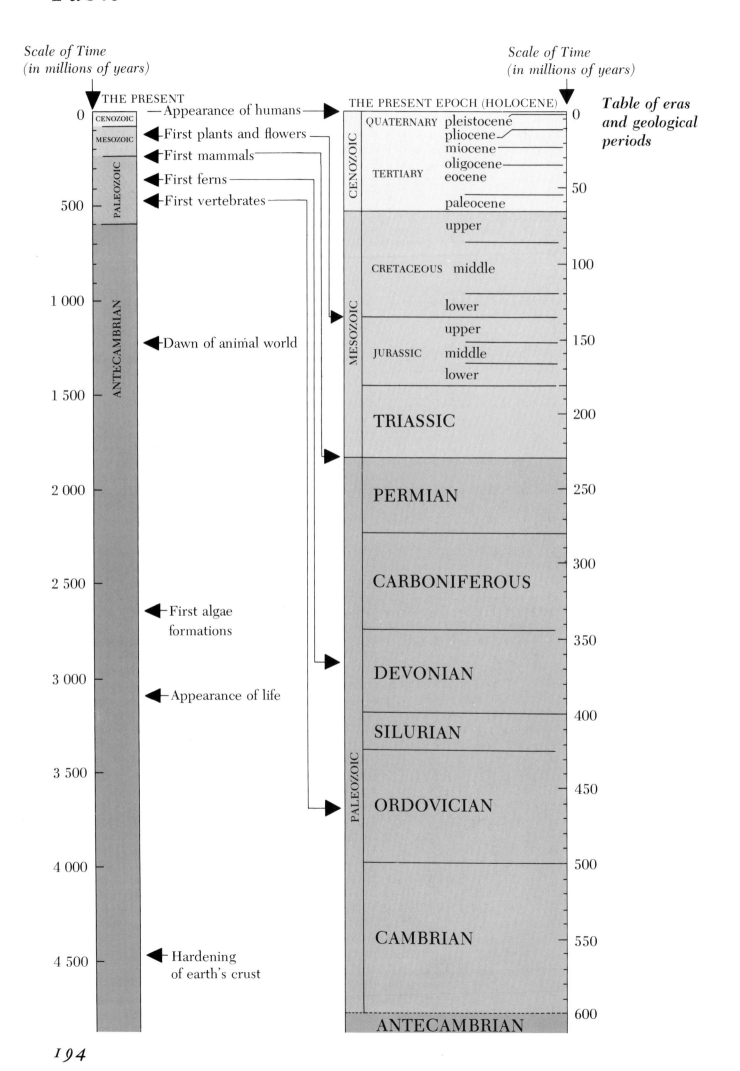

THE PRESENT

0

CENOZOIC

MESOZOIC

PALEOZOIC

500

ANTECAMBRIAN

1 000

1 500

2 000

2 500

3 000

3 500

4 000

4 500

— Appearance of humans

First plants and flowers

First mammals

First ferns

First vertebrates

Dawn of animal world

First algae
formations

Appearance of life

Hardening
of earth's crust

THE PRESENT EPOCH (HOLOCENE)

0

*Table of eras
and geological
periods*

CENOZOIC

QUATERNARY   pleistocene
pliocene
miocene
TERTIARY   oligocene
eocene

paleocene

50

upper

CRETACEOUS   middle

100

lower

upper

JURASSIC   middle

150

lower

TRIASSIC

200

MESOZOIC

PERMIAN

250

CARBONIFEROUS

300

350

DEVONIAN

SILURIAN

400

PALEOZOIC

ORDOVICIAN

450

500

CAMBRIAN

550

600

ANTECAMBRIAN

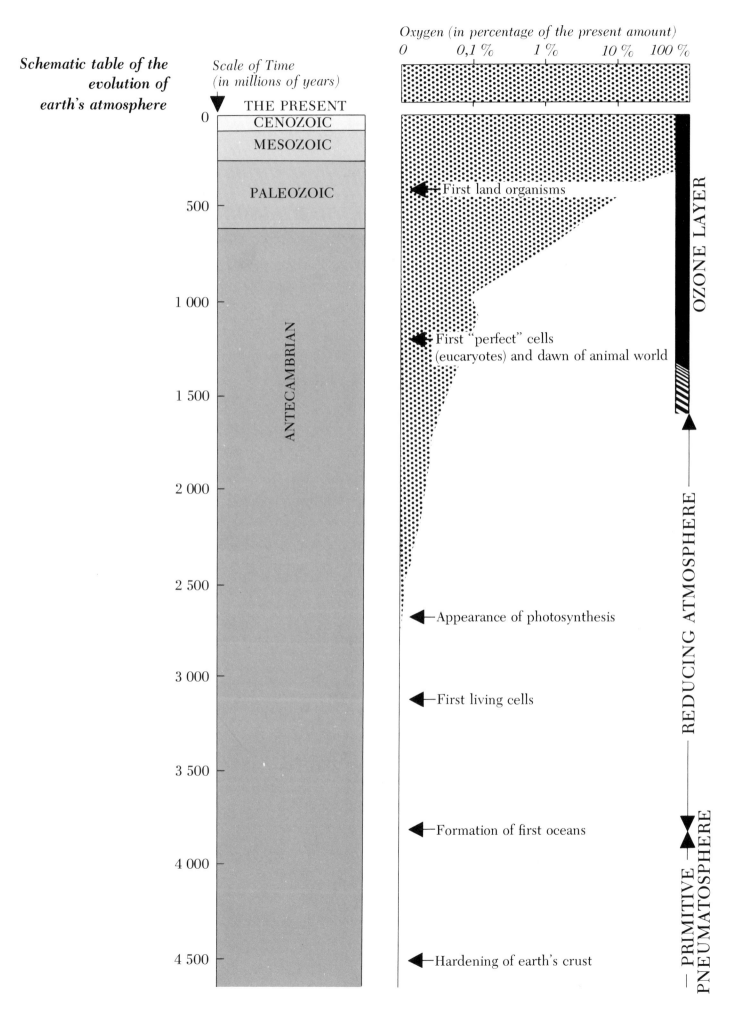

Schematic table of the evolution of earth's atmosphere

Scale of Time
(in millions of years)

THE PRESENT

0

CENOZOIC

MESOZOIC

PALEOZOIC

500

1 000

ANTECAMBRIAN

1 500

2 000

2 500

3 000

3 500

4 000

4 500

Oxygen (in percentage of the present amount)

0   0,1 %   1 %   10 %   100 %

First land organisms

First "perfect" cells
(eucaryotes) and dawn of animal world

Appearance of photosynthesis

First living cells

Formation of first oceans

Hardening of earth's crust

OZONE LAYER

REDUCING ATMOSPHERE

PRIMITIVE PNEUMATOSPHERE

Index

*The numbers refer to page numbers.
Numbers in parentheses refer to
plates outside the text.*

S

T

V W Z

Bibliography

Alimen, H. 1950. *Atlas de préhistoire.* 3 vols. Paris: Boubée et Cie.

Aubouin, J., Brosse, R., Lehman, J.-P. 1975. *Précis de géologie. II, Paléontologie stratigraphique.* Paris: Dunod Editions.

Augusta, J. 1963. *A Book of Mammouth.* London: P. Hamlyn Editions.

Babin, C. 1971. *Eléments de paléontologie.* Paris: Armand Colin Editions.

Boule, M., Piveteau, J. 1935. *Les fossiles: Eléments de paléontologie.* Paris: Masson et Cie.

Boureau, E. 1960. *Traité de paléobotanique.* 9 vols. Paris: Masson et Cie.

Chavan, A., Cailleux, A. 1957. *Détermination pratique des fossiles.* Paris: Masson et Cie.

Chavan, A., Montocchio, H. 1968. *Fossiles classiques.* Paris: Deyrolle Editions.

Colbert, E. H. 1968. *Dinosaurs: Their Discovery and Their World.* New York: Dutton and Co.

Deflandre, G. 1971. *La vie créatrice de roches.* Paris: Presses Universitaires de France.

Denizot, G. 1971–76. *Atlas de fossiles.* 3 vols. Paris: N. Boubée Editions.

Easton, W. H. 1960. *Invertebrate Paleontology.* New York: Harper & Bros.

Emberger, L. 1968. *Les plantes fossiles dans leurs rapports avec les végétaux vivants.* Paris: Masson et Cie.

Furon, R. 1943. *La paléontologie: La science des fossiles, son histoire, ses enseignements, ses curiosités.* Paris: Pavot Editions.

Genet-Varcin, E. 1969. *A la recherche du primate, ancêtre de l'homme.* Paris: Boubée et Cie.

Gignoux, M. 1950. *Géologie stratigraphique.* Paris: Masson et Cie.

Hamilton, W. R., Woolley, A. R., Bishop, A. C. 1974. *Les minéraux, roches et fossiles.* Paris: Elsevier Editions.

Kirkaldy, J. F. 1975. *Les fossiles en couleurs.* Paris: Fernand Nathan Editions.

Kurten, B. 1968. *Le monde des dinosaures.* Paris: Hatchette Editions.

Lehman, J.-P. 1973. Les preuves paléontologiques de l'évolution. Paris: Presses Universitaires de France.

Moore, R. C., Lalicker, C. G., Fischer, A. G. 1952. *Invertebrate Fossils.* New York: McGraw-Hill.

Moret, L. 1966. *Manuel de paléontologie animale.* Paris: Masson et Cie.

Petersen, K. 1973. *Les animaux préhistoriques.* Paris: Fernand Nathan Editions.

Pinna, G. 1973. *Les fossiles invertébrés.* Grange Batelière Editions.

Pinna, G. 1974. *Les fossiles.* Paris: Robert Laffont Editions.

Piveteau, J. 1952–57. Traité de paléontologie. 7 vols. Paris: Masson et Cie.

Pomerol, C. 1968–76. *Guides géologiques régionaux.* Paris: Masson et Cie.

Pomerol, C. 1973. *Stratigraphie et paléogéographie: Ere cénozoïque.* Paris: Doin Editions.

Rasmussen, W. 1969. *Palaeontologie: Fossile invertebrater.* Copenhagen: Munksgaad Editions.

Rhodes, F. M., Zim, H. S., Shaffer, P. R. 1975. *Fossiles.* Paris: Hachette Editions.

Roger, J. 1974. *Paléontologie générale.* Paris: Masson et Cie.

Romer, A. S. 1959. *The Vertebrate Body.* Philadelphia: W. B. Saunders Co.

Romer, A. S. 1966. *Vertebrate Paleontology.* Chicago and London: University of Chicago Press.

Schindewolf, O. H. 1950. *Grundfragen des Paläontologie.* Stuttgart: Schweirerbart'sche Edition.

Seward, A. C. 1959. *Plant Life Through the Ages.* New York: Hafner Publishers.

Spinar, Z. 1965. *Systematika paleontology bezobratlych.* Academia Praha.

Spinar, Z. 1973. *Encyclopédie de la préhistoire.* Paris: La Farandole.

Swinnerton, H. H. 1960. Fossils. London: Collins Editions.

Termier, H. and Termier, G. 1960. *Paléontologie stratigraphique.* Paris: Masson et Cie.

Termier, H. and Termier, G. 1968. *Biologie et écologie des premiers fossiles.* Paris: Masson et Cie.

Fossils of All Ages

Printed in 1978.
All the fossils illustrated in this book are from the collection of the National Museum of Natural History, Paris. The photographs were taken by Denis Serrette and Rachid Kandaroun, except for the following:
Nos. 10, 14, 15, 16, 17, 63, 64, 65: Library of the Museum, Paris.
Nos. 11, 54: Museum of Man, Paris.
No. 51: Y. Reyre.
Nos. 52, 53, 57, 58, 120, 121, 123: G. Deflandre.
No. 56: D. Noel.
No. 90: J. P. Caulet.